# THE *D*REAM MASTER

MAHANTA

This book has been authored by and published under the supervision of the Mahanta, the Living ECK Master, Sri Harold Klemp. It is the Word of ECK.

# THE DREAM MASTER

## HAROLD KLEMP

MAHANTA TRANSCRIPTS

BOOK 8

ECKANKAR
Minneapolis

**The Dream Master,** Mahanta Transcripts, Book 8

Copyright © 1993, 1997 ECKANKAR

Printed in U.S.A.
Second Edition — 1997

Compiled by Joan Klemp and Anne Pezdirc
Edited by Anthony Moore and Mary Carroll Moore
Text Illustrations by Fraser MacDonald
Text photo (page xii) by Mike Steinberg
Back cover photo by Robert Huntley

Publisher's Cataloging in Publication
*(Prepared by Quality Books Inc.)*

Klemp, Harold.
    The dream master / Harold Klemp. — 2nd ed.
    p. cm. — (Mahanta transcripts ; bk. 8)
    Includes index.
    ISBN: 1-57043-009-8

    1. Eckankar. I. Title. II. Series: Klemp, Harold. Mahanta transcripts ; bk. 8.

BP605.E3K554 1997                     299'.93
                                       QBI95-20524

# Contents

# FOREWORD

The teachings of ECK define the nature of Soul. You are Soul, a particle of God sent into the worlds (including earth) to gain spiritual experience.

The goal in ECK is spiritual freedom in this lifetime, after which you become a Co-worker with God, both here and in the next world. Karma and reincarnation are primary beliefs.

Key to the ECK teachings is the Mahanta, the Living ECK Master. He has the special ability to act as both the Inner and Outer Master for ECK students. He is the prophet of Eckankar, given respect but not worship. He teaches the sacred name of God, HU, which lifts you spiritually into the Light and Sound of God, the ECK. Purified by the practice of the Spiritual Exercises of ECK, you are then able to accept the full love of God in this lifetime.

Sri Harold Klemp is the Mahanta, the Living ECK Master. He has written many books, discourses, and articles about the spiritual life. Many of his public talks are available on audio- and videocassette. His teachings uplift people and help them recognize and understand their own experiences in the Light and Sound of God.

*The Dream Master,* Mahanta Transcripts, Book 8, is a collection of Sri Harold's talks from 1988 to 1989. May they serve to uplift you on your journey home to God.

At the 1989 ECK Springtime Seminar in San Diego, Sri Harold Klemp, the Mahanta, the Living ECK Master explains how dreams help you learn to recognize truth and discover divine meaning in your life.

# 1

# THE DREAM MASTER, PART 1

*S*leep is a wonderful rejuvenator, and in ECK it is enhanced by the Dream Master.

A popular myth in ECK is that the Living ECK Master never requires more than four hours of sleep a night. Some people take their myths very seriously, so I have to be careful how I dispel this one. The fact is, I get a normal amount of sleep.

As a child, there were many nights when I would be afraid to go to sleep. I would lay awake for hours listening to the strange sounds, wondering if the night would ever end. This fear of the night lingered to some extent even as I grew older. Only after I came in contact with the teachings of ECK and Paul Twitchell did I discover that sleep had a significance beyond resting the body.

## WHY ARE WE HERE?

Terrill Willson's book, *How I Learned Soul Travel,* is a wonderful example of the effort a person will put forth to move into higher states of awareness. Whether we know it or not, the reason we are here is to try to reach a higher state of spiritual consciousness.

*Whether we know it or not, the reason we are here is to try to reach a higher state of spiritual consciousness.*

Through the Dream Master you become more acquainted with yourself as a spiritual being who happens to wear a physical body. This expanded viewpoint makes you more highly attuned to the operation of the physical body. You learn things about your diet or other habits that keep you from functioning well, that cause you to feel uncomfortable or to get a cold or sore throat. Often, though not always, these conditions can be prevented.

*Through the Dream Master you become more acquainted with yourself as a spiritual being who happens to wear a physical body.*

As a youngster I liked chocolate a lot—devil's food cake, chocolate candy, anything I could get my hands on. I also used to have a lot of toothaches, but I didn't connect them to my eating habits. I just thought they were part of life.

Later I began to see in the dream state that what I ate had a very definite effect on how I felt. Eating habits affect health.

## SIMPLE, BUT EFFECTIVE

When I look at the ECK teachings on dreams, sometimes I feel almost apologetic. They're not clever or trendy. They are simple, active teachings: You, by your own will, decide to explore your inner life to learn more about your outer life.

A few ECK initiates in the Minneapolis area conducted a workshop on dreams at a local campus. One student-reporter for the university newspaper looked in on the meeting and apparently didn't find it exciting enough. He wrote an article to the effect that he had checked out the ECK teachings on dreams and hadn't seen much to recommend them. His article included quotes by several experts at the university. They used all the latest buzzwords to describe their cleverly put-together programs on dream interpretation. The student was obviously impressed by their approach. What he failed to see was that the ECK teachings are effective and they work—year after year.

## ONE-TO-ONE

Some ECKists have difficulty remembering their dreams, but others are very aware of working with the Dream Master. This is a very real being, someone not generally known in the more contemporary teachings on dreams. People outside of ECK who hear of the Dream Master try to fit him into some kind of symbology: "Oh, yes, he represents your inner urgings and strivings to reach satisfaction and happiness, and therefore, blah, blah, blah."

They don't understand, of course, that the Mahanta, the Living ECK Master is the Dream Master and that he can work with you on a one-to-one basis. He can help you understand the attitudes that affect your health and bring insight into problems you may be having with others.

*The Dream Master can help you understand the attitudes that affect your health and bring insight into problems you may be having with others.*

## PAST LIVES

When people seem to be coming at you from all directions, sometimes you can't help wondering, *Why do I have to go through an experience like this?* But because the ECK teachings take into consideration the role of karma, eventually you come to a greater understanding of these things.

Many of the contemporary dream teachings, trying to work from a Christian background, do not recognize the effect of karma, and so they ignore it. Their explanations disregard the feelings and impulses that have been created in the past, sometimes in the far, distant past of another lifetime.

Any study of dreams that is based merely on the

happenings of this lifetime or on a product of the mind such as symbols, without taking into account past lives, is superficial. Most dream teachings of contemporary western culture are shallow and have very little to offer people besides glitter.

A number of people who work in these fields would respond, "Yes, but even with the limitations, one can learn to understand himself a little better than he did before he began to study his dreams under our methods and techniques." And I would have to agree with them. There is an elementary stage to the study of dreams, and this is the area the other people are covering.

*The teachings of ECK, which include the study of dreams, continue where the others leave off.*

The teachings of ECK, which include the study of dreams, are the advanced teachings. We continue where the others leave off. But we continue in such a natural, low-key way that other people may not recognize that we have something special, something unique. Nothing that you or I can say will convince them that there is a unique feature to the dream teachings of ECK.

The first part of these teachings is the Dream Master. He usually appears in the form of the current Living ECK Master. Often he is accompanied by other ECK Masters that ECKists have come to know, such as Yaubl Sacabi, Lai Tsi, Fubbi Quantz, Rebazar Tarzs, and Peddar Zaskq, whom we also know as Paul Twitchell.

## WAKE-UP CALL

To some, the ECK dream teachings seem almost too humble, yet this is how the ECK works. A dream experience can be as simple as a wake-up call. I used to hear a knocking sound, as if someone had rapped sharply on the door to my room. It would happen about forty-five minutes to an hour before my alarm clock was set to wake me for work. The sound was so clear that, as I gradually came back to the physical body, I actually thought someone had knocked on my door. But when I got up and opened the door to look, no one was there.

It usually happened that the knock interrupted one of my inner experiences. Since there was still time before I had to get ready for work, I could take the opportunity to write down the dream while the memory was fresh.

The knocking frightened me at first; I didn't know who was doing it or what was happening. Eventually I realized it was the Dream Master and that he was saying, "I have given you an experience on the other planes that has meaning for you. I want you to remember it. Wake up and write it down." The wake-up call gave me the time and opportunity to record whatever had come through.

Soon I stopped questioning the knocking and whatever other means the Dream Master used to awaken me. When it came, I just got up, opened my dream journal, and wrote down what had occurred in the dream state.

## DREAM CENSOR

I also found that the Dream Master often works through the Etheric mind. A portion of the Etheric mind has an automatic function which operates as the censor. If the Etheric mind feels that a certain experience in the other worlds will be too much of a shock to the dreamer, the censor comes in, says, "Shut it down!"—and wipes out the dream.

The censor may make you forget the dream. This accounts for the times you wake up knowing that

*A portion of the Etheric mind has an automatic function which operates as the censor.*

something happened, that it was important, but you can't quite remember it. It's like a writer struggling to come up with a certain word or a musician trying to find the right note—you know it's there, but you can't quite get it. In the same way, you cannot quite grasp the dream experience you know you had.

## TRANSLATOR FUNCTION

There is also a higher part of the Etheric mind, which corresponds to the high Mental Plane. This is the level at which the Dream Master works. The Dream Master translates or converts an experience in the other worlds into symbols or words that you can understand here. I call this the translator function.

*There is also a higher part of the Etheric mind, the level at which the Dream Master works.*

Different languages or modes of communication are used on some of the other planes. As the communication comes through the Etheric mind, it is unscrambled and retranslated for your physical mind. All the ideas expressed in the other planes are then perceived in the language you normally speak here on earth.

There are modes of transportation in some of the other planes which we cannot fathom here. For instance, vehicles may be propelled without wheels, in ways that the human mind simply can't understand. Things like this are unscrambled and converted into something we can relate to.

*The Dream Master gives you an experience in another world because there is a lesson for you to learn.*

The Dream Master gives you an experience in another world because there is a lesson for you to learn. It may have to do with a harmful habit or attitude you have acquired, such as anger. The Dream Master will guide you in the Soul body to another plane for an experience that will point out the harm your attitude is causing you.

In ECK, your experiences are no longer limited

to your daily, waking life. The Dream Master expands your experience to give you an opportunity to gain spiritual unfoldment twenty-four hours a day, whether you are awake or in the dream state.

There would be no point to the message from the Dream Master if all you got out of it was, Oh, look at the funny machines and how strange the people talk. These things are run through the upper Etheric mind and unscrambled. Speech and objects in the other world are converted to correspond to something that makes sense to the human consciousness. A vehicle that moves without wheels there might be translated to the physical mind as a car with wheels. Without this translator function, the experience would be lost.

To summarize this as simply as possible: The lower part of the Etheric mind is a censor, and the higher part is an unscrambler. It unscrambles the incomprehensible and makes it something that your physical consciousness can accept.

## NIGHTMARES

The lower Etheric censor aids and abets the human mind in an attempt to protect you from experiences it feels would shock or confuse you. If a spiritual message is coming through from the Dream Master to you in the human consciousness, the lower Etheric mind, which normally acts as a censor of high spiritual truths, generally tries to let it come through as a nightmare.

There is a constant battle going on between the spiritual and the negative powers. The Dream Master then must try to undo the damage of this nightmare, caused by the censor scrambling an inner experience and letting it come through to frighten you.

*The Dream Master expands your experience to give you an opportunity to gain spiritual unfoldment twenty-four hours a day.*

## OPPOSING FORCES

In ECK, as we go further in the study of dreams, we find that there is a conflict of opposing forces going on in the inner worlds just like here in the physical world.

*There is a conflict of opposing forces going on in the inner worlds just like here in the physical world.*

For example, say you have a goal to buy a car. Before you know it, all sorts of obstacles come up to oppose your desire to buy the car. Perhaps you have a teenager in the family who says, "Oh, boy, I can't wait to get behind the wheel to see how fast it can go!"

Now you have serious misgivings about having a new car in the family. It looks like you may never get to use it, and you fear that it will get scratched up with your teenager at the wheel. That is one conflict, one opposing force, that goes into motion as you try to reach what you feel is the positive goal of buying a car.

Other opposition may also occur. You have just enough money saved for the down payment. You go to the car dealer and try to make a deal. He suggests you apply for a loan through the bank, which sometimes presents a whole new set of obstacles.

All of a sudden the water heater bursts or the roof starts to leak. The money you had set aside for the down payment on the car has to be used for this essential repair. Setback! Now you either have to wait several more months until you can save up more money, or you have to depend on more creative financing.

In other words, here in the physical world, Soul — which means you in the human body — has a desire. It wants something in order to be happy. So you set a goal, make plans to achieve it, and then everything that possibly can get between you and your goal occurs.

The same kind of opposition happens in your dream state. The spiritual powers constantly try to come to you through the direction of the Dream Master. He wants to bring you insights for your spiritual benefit, to make you a greater and better person. On the other hand there are the negative forces which may be, among other things, your subconscious fears from past lives.

Negative experiences are the testing ground of Soul. They are there purposely for you to overcome. The Dream Master can overcome some nightmares for you, but he may not always take care of the entire nightmare. In some instances, you may be facing a karmic debt that you created many years ago. It is better to work it out in the dream state than to have this karmic debt appear in your physical life.

*Negative experiences are the testing ground of Soul.*

## WAS IT A DREAM?

Some dream experiences are simple. They won't always make you stand up and shout, "Wow, that was a really big experience!" Yet you know it was a valid inner experience.

You may even be a little frightened the first time it happens. Simple experiences such as the wake-up call are perceived right on the border of your consciousness. You usually assume it's out here in the physical world. You haven't figured out yet that it was an inner call.

As you go higher in your dream study, at times it's going to be hard to tell the physical and the dream world apart. It may be difficult to distinguish whether something happened in the dream or out here. Eventually you find that everything in the lower worlds is a dream. It's all a dream.

## RIGHT ON TIME

An individual planned to go to an ECK seminar. She and her husband had been out very late the night before they were to leave, and she was concerned that they would oversleep. When she finally got into bed at two-thirty in the morning, she asked the Dream Master, "Please help me get up by seven o'clock so that I can get to the train station in time."

She had been asleep for a few hours when suddenly she was jolted awake by the doorbell ringing. She tried to ignore it and go back to sleep. But it rang over and over, making a horrible racket.

"Who's there?" she called out. Nobody answered, but the ringing continued.

Very agitated by now, she jumped up, ran to the door, and jerked it open. She was quite surprised to find that no one was there. On her way back to the bedroom, she glanced at the clock and saw that it was one minute after seven. She realized she had gotten her wake-up call right on schedule.

Some people not in ECK have similar experiences and misunderstand them. They say, "An evil force is trying to enter my life!" They do not recognize that it is a good force working in their behalf.

*The Dream Master will come when you ask. You first have to learn to ask, and then you have to learn to recognize when he speaks.*

## YOU HAVE TO LEARN TO ASK

The wake-up call came to the ECKist because she had asked. This is important to know: The Dream Master will come when you ask. You first have to learn to ask, and then you have to learn to recognize when he speaks. Our whole concern in ECK is how to become more conscious individuals; to become more conscious of who and what we are.

## WASTEBASKET TECHNIQUE

An ECKist started a new job as a music teacher in an elementary school. At first she was very excited about teaching the students how to sing and play the instruments.

But soon she found that working with the children day after day was becoming quite a strain. "I'm always so tired," she complained to the other teachers. "I feel under such pressure."

"That's to be expected when you give so much to the children," an older, more experienced teacher told her. "Not only are you attempting to teach them how to sing and play the instruments, you're trying to wake them up to something beautiful, to instill enthusiasm in them. This takes a toll on you. You're going to continue to be exhausted until you learn how to work with it."

One night she fell asleep and met with the Dream Master, the inner being ECKists know as Wah Z. He took her into his office. "Take your cares and worries and throw them in here," he instructed her, pointing to the wastebasket. She did.

She awoke in the morning feeling more rested and better than she had in quite a while. The mood stayed with her throughout the day. The idea of dreaming was very much on her mind. During one class the fifth-graders were singing a song about daydreams. She suddenly felt inspired to ask them, "How many of you remember your dreams?"

Ten hands went up.

"Do any of you ever try to change your dreams?" she asked.

Several of the children were eager to tell her about their dream experiences. It became apparent to her that some of them were learning how to work

*You are the creator in your dream worlds, whether they are on the inner planes or out here in the physical.*

with their dream state. If something unpleasant was happening, they attempted to change it.

## USING YOUR CREATIVITY

You are the creator in your dream worlds, whether they are on the inner planes or out here in the physical. The Dream Master tries to show you how to use your creativity, how to make your life better out here because of what you learned on the inner planes.

This simple teaching is often overlooked by people who ask for help. "Oh, please, Master," they'll say, "take away this problem." Sometimes it's, "Dear Master, please get me some money," or, "I have this wonderful plan. If you can make it pay off, then I will give 10 percent of the profits to Eckankar."

It's a bribe, of course. They figure if they talk sweetly to the Inner Master, the Mahanta, he will say, "That's really swell of you. Sure, we could use 10 percent of your fortune. I'll see that you get it." It never occurs to these people that if the Mahanta needed money, he wouldn't have to go through an intermediary.

## BEAUTIFUL SOUL

After the students had discussed their dreams, the teacher had them sing a song which has a line that goes something like, "You see the wonderful and beautiful person who you are." She noticed that the boys weren't singing along. Then she realized the reason for their reluctance: They were uncomfortable singing a song in which they had to call themselves beautiful. To boys that age, of course, beautiful equals sissy or unmanly.

"The song doesn't refer to you as boys or girls," she explained. "We are singing about you as Soul. You are Soul, and as Soul you are beautiful." She began the song again, and this time, the boys sang along.

The dream teachings of ECK allowed this teacher to get rid of some of her daily cares and worries by putting them into the Master's waste-basket. With her own burden lifted, she was able to recognize the individuality of the children. She saw a dimension to their learning that went beyond the normal curriculum. She could see the side of them which rarely shows itself in the daytime— she could see their dream self. She could see they were more than just children; they were beautiful, eternal beings.

## WAYSHOWER

Many people, not acquainted with the simplicity of ECK, mock the teachings in favor of methods that seem more sophisticated but essentially are very shallow. I constantly look for some way to get through to you, the dreamer, and especially to those of you who are having a difficult time with your dream studies.

*The Wayshower can show each of you your own way home to God.*

I always come back to the definition of the Mahanta, the Living ECK Master as a Wayshower. He is not a way-pusher or a way-dragger who kicks and shoves you through the inner worlds. The Wayshower is, quite simply, someone who shows the way.

He can show each of you your own way home to God. He can guide you through the inner worlds, pointing out where it is safe to go and where it is not so safe to go. But he can be a Wayshower only to those who recognize him and listen to his instructions for working in the dream state.

## ARE YOU READY?

I cannot force people into a direction they don't want to go. If they don't want to go that way, they just won't go. Yet, I feel a certain responsibility when someone writes to me and says, "I'm getting nowhere. I'm not making any progress."

Sometimes it's just as well that they aren't going anywhere in the dream state, because they aren't ready. If you move too fast, before you're ready, it can be an upsetting experience.

For some people, it's like trying to sky dive. They may have the desire to do it, but the first few times they attempt to jump out of the plane, they freeze up. What if the parachute doesn't open? For the time being, they feel much safer on land.

Not everybody is prepared for an experience like the inner sky dive. It's too far removed from what they are used to doing. You have to build up to these things.

## INNER PEER PRESSURE

Another form of anxiety is caused by peer pressure, real or imagined. You may hear someone else talking about his dramatic experiences in the inner planes. Actually, he may never have had a real experience with the Sound and Light of God. But you don't want to be left out. Others are doing it, you think, so you'd better do it too. Whether you are ready or not, you timidly say, "Yes, I would like to Soul Travel and have a wonderful experience."

*Sometimes all that people need is one experience. It will last a lifetime.*

But you have to work up to this. Not always, of course; it's not the same with everybody. But for each of us, the time has to be right. Sometimes all that people need is one experience. It will last a lifetime. It gives them all the proof they need that there is life beyond this narrow physical existence. It settles within them the question Is there more to life than what I can see and feel? It gives them what they need to begin creating a life in which they can be happy.

Fear is usually what holds the dreamer back from remembering travel in the other worlds. Generally it is not a fear that has been gained in this lifetime. It comes from a past lifetime. The Spiritual Exercises of ECK lead you into the dream world, where the Dream Master shows you a number of ways to confront your fears.

*Fear is usually what holds the dreamer back from remembering travel in the other worlds.*

## SPIRITUAL GEOGRAPHY

The Dream Master is one with the Outer Master. It is the Outer Master who provides the books and teachings of ECK so that you can gain some understanding of the geography of the inner worlds. He does this so you are not caught off guard when something happens on the inner planes, even if it is not exactly as described in the ECK books. You have enough information to say, "I have a feeling I was on the Mental Plane," or, "I went into a setting that was definitely from a past life. I was operating from the Causal Plane."

The ECK teachings give you enough spiritual geography to explain where you have been and why. This allows you to put your mind to rest. The reason people without the ECK background are often upset by their inner experiences is because they have no way to fit them into anything society considers normal. They cannot relate them to what we in ECK know is spiritually normal.

When an individual has an experience that places him outside the herd, that makes him feel separate from the masses, he feels uncomfortable. It is human nature to want to belong. Through the dream teachings of ECK, we learn that we can belong, but now it is with a higher order of beings. We can belong to a group of spiritual beings who operate both in the physical and the invisible worlds.

## MAGGIE AND THOR

It is quite natural to move back and forth between the planes in full consciousness, to see different places, and to converse with beings who have the great wisdom of God. Furthermore, it is a sign that you are moving ahead spiritually in very fine fashion.

An ECK initiate was in the habit of doing her spiritual exercises each night in the living room. She would sit on the floor, her two large dogs nearby, then close her eyes and sing HU, the love song to God.

Fortunately, her dogs, Maggie and Thor, always sat quietly as she sang "HU-U-U-U." They didn't try to help by howling along. This could be quite a distraction, especially if the dogs weigh a hundred pounds each.

The woman's husband finally finished remodeling the attic, which he had made into their bedroom. It was such a pretty room, she decided this was where she'd now do her spiritual exercises.

The first night she and the dogs went up to her new attic bedroom, she noticed a peculiar thing. As soon as she sat down and began to sing HU, Thor and Maggie left the room. The same thing happened the next night and the next. She couldn't understand why. The two dogs always followed her wherever she went and stayed right with her. But something had changed.

One night she went into her new bedroom and began the Spiritual Exercises of ECK to strengthen

*We can belong to a group of spiritual beings who operate both in the physical and the invisible worlds.*

her connection with the inner worlds. Once again, as soon as she closed her eyes and started to chant HU, she heard the dogs run out of the room.

*Am I singing HU in the wrong key?* she wondered. *Did the dogs change their minds and decide they don't want to do the spiritual exercises anymore?*

People who aren't in ECK may not realize that some of their pets are more than just animals who make a racket at feeding time or get underfoot and make a nuisance of themselves. Many of the pets that come into the homes of the ECKists are very high spiritual beings. They too know and appreciate the beauty of this love song to God, the HU.

One night she decided to find out what was going on. As usual, the dogs followed her upstairs to the bedroom. She began to chant HU, the dogs dashed out of the room, and this time she followed them. They headed down the stairs and straight to the living room. As she watched them get comfortable in their favorite spot and shut their eyes, she suddenly realized what was happening. Her chanting signaled the start of the spiritual exercises, and the dogs came down to their established place in the living room so they could do theirs too.

I guess the moral of this story is, if the dogs in ECK can do their spiritual exercises, so can you.

## Two Forces

I wanted to discuss the lower (censor) and higher (translator) aspects of the Etheric mind because I thought you might find it interesting as you work with the two forces within yourself, the spiritual and the negative. Both forces are from God, the Sugmad.

In ECK we understand that the negative powers are there to temper Soul. Perhaps the other religions

*In ECK we understand that the negative powers are there to temper Soul.*

will learn eventually that the evil power, being subordinate to the divine power of God, must be here for a purpose; otherwise it would not be allowed to survive. Its purpose is to temper Soul. It's that simple.

*You are growing into your own divinity.*

If you are confronted by negative things and are inspired to exert the spiritual rather than the negative force within yourself, then you have gained in spiritual unfoldment. You have become more a son or daughter of God. You are growing into your own divinity.

## INTO THE LIGHT

I would like to give a technique that will help if you have a dream that you don't like. Close your eyes and go into contemplation for about fifteen minutes.

Begin by chanting HU—one of the most beautiful words in the language of mankind. After you have chanted HU for a few minutes, rewind the dream that upset you or that left you somewhere you didn't want to be. Run through the dream mentally, from the beginning up to the point where you awoke. Then try to take it one step further.

Perhaps the dream ended with you in a frightening situation—let's say a dark basement. In your spiritual exercise, take it to the point where you were left in the dark basement. Then use your imaginative faculty to get yourself out of there: Visualize an open door that leads to golden sunlight. Know that this golden light is the Light of Divine Spirit, the Light of ECK, the Light of God. Look to the Light, and listen for the Sound.

Remember, when you have a dream that you would like to change, you can go into contemplation and use this technique to take the dream one step further. Always take it to a higher level. Move it out of the darkness, out of the silence and loneliness. Take it to the Light and Sound of God.

Through this Spiritual Exercise of ECK, you are creating for yourself an open door to a greater world. Soon you will find that you have established a new habit. When you run into dark and troubling times, awake or asleep, you will be in the habit of creating for yourself a brighter world in which you can be happier and more satisfied than you were before.

If you can achieve an improvement over yesterday, even a small one, then you have gained significantly. You, with the help of the Dream Master, have done it yourself. You are taking charge of your own world because you are becoming a creator.

*Through this Spiritual Exercise of ECK, you are creating for yourself an open door to a greater world.*

*ECK Worldwide Seminar, Atlanta, Georgia, Friday, October 21, 1988*

In numerous ways, the Mahanta tries to show you the
kernels of truth, those precious gems lying all around you.

# 2
# THE DREAM
# MASTER, PART 2

*A* few of us were in an elevator when it stopped between floors. A young man on the elevator with us began to sweat. He frantically pressed the buttons to go up, down, anywhere—but every time we got the door a few inches open, all we saw was a big block of brown concrete.

## THE SECRET LATCH

Another person happened to know that there was a secret latch that would open the doors all the way. He ran his hand along the side of one of the sliding doors until he found the latch, and in just a few seconds he got it open. We found that the elevator had stopped some four feet above the floor, so we all had to bend over and jump down to get out of there. I thought it went very smoothly.

When it came the young man's turn, he jumped out too. But his last comment as he headed for the stairway was, "That's sca-a-ry!" The rest of us just got on the other elevator.

To me it was an interesting experience. The elevator got stuck, but someone knew what to do about it. There was a way to resolve the problem—the secret latch—and once he found it, everything was instantly OK.

## AWARENESS OF TRUTH

The physical world as well as the inner planes can all rightly be considered the dream world. Truth reveals itself to us constantly, even here in the physical world. But how many people are aware of it? Not too many.

Occasionally something occurs that I call the Golden-tongued Wisdom, where the Mahanta warns you to watch out for something about to happen in your everyday life. The warning gives you the opportunity to be alert so you can protect yourself.

## FRESHNESS DATE

An ECKist went to the store to buy milk. She took her time, carefully examining the freshness date stamped on each carton. Just then an old man came over and stood next to her. "You MUST check the freshness date!" he said. When she didn't respond, he became very vehement about it. "You absolutely MUST check that freshness date!" That's exactly what she had planned to do, until someone told her she *had* to do it.

Glaring defiantly at the old man, she reached into the cooler and picked up a carton that had the second freshest date. Nobody was going to tell *her* what to do.

The next morning she got up early to make breakfast for her family. As usual, she turned on the radio to listen to the news as she cooked. One particular report suddenly caught her attention. The Health Department had issued an alert: certain cartons of milk had been found to be contaminated and should not be used. The report went on to identify the cartons in question.

The woman immediately went to the refrigerator and took out her carton of milk. Sure enough, the one she had bought—with the second freshest date—was contaminated. She was given a second chance to catch it before she served it to her family.

This is one example of how the Mahanta works through the Golden-tongued Wisdom. The ECKist was given a warning through the words of the old man, who for no reason at all felt compelled to tell her, "You must check the freshness date."

## PRECIOUS GEMS

Her initial reaction was almost predictable, though. Most ECKists are quite independent by nature. If someone says, "Go left," they are likely to say, "Thanks for the information," and go right. And when they turn right and everything goes wrong, they'll say, "Why didn't the Mahanta warn me?"

The Mahanta does warn. He does teach. In numerous ways, he tries to show you the kernels of truth, those precious gems lying all around you. The physical plane is loaded with these gems of truth. We literally kick our way through them as we walk around in our daily life every day. And as we walk through them, there is this pathway to show where we have gone.

*The physical plane is loaded with these gems of truth.*

But often as we go through life, we are neither aware of the gems nor of our path up to that point in life. We rarely look behind us to see where we stand, so that we can see where we are today.

## EFFECT OF INTERFERENCE

One of the initiates has a habit of interfering in other people's space, and she recognizes this. She isn't the only one with such problems. As we begin on the path of ECK and move into the higher stages, we have to keep our eyes open and learn to recognize in our own lives the spiritual principles that are being taught to us by the Mahanta.

Her lesson from the Dream Master came in two parts. In the first dream, she was the person who was offended; in the second, she was the offender. The Inner Master, or the Dream Master, was simply trying to show her the importance of allowing other people their spiritual space. This means that we do not interfere, eavesdrop, or any of those other things we feel we have the right to do. We do not have the right to meddle in other people's personal business.

In the first dream, she was seated at a table in a restaurant. The Dream Master, Wah Z, was talking with a group of people nearby. At one point he leaned across the table and began to speak directly to her. But as he was talking to the dreamer, giving her kernels of wisdom and truth, someone at the table interrupted him. She waited for Wah Z to go on, but instead he sat back in his chair and said, "Well, that's all I have to say anyway." But she knew better. He had stopped speaking because someone else had interrupted his message.

One can readily accept a dream like this, where someone else is the wrongdoer. She didn't quite connect it to her own habits yet. But a few days later she had another inner experience to show how she was often the offender.

In the dream world, she was standing near the front of a long line of people who were waiting to say hello to Wah Z. Each person would shake Wah Z's hand, exchange a few words with him, and move on so that the others in line could have their turn.

The dreamer's turn finally came, and she shook his hand. But instead of moving on to allow others their chance to have a private word with him, she stood at his elbow and listened in on his conversations with the initiates he was now greeting.

As she eavesdropped and imposed her own opinions on several people who had each come to ask Wah Z for a spiritual healing, the higher part of the Etheric mind went into action. This is the part that translates inner experiences into graphic images that the dreamer will certainly remember and, hopefully, learn where he or she went wrong.

One of the initiates was holding some human organs in his hands. The Dream Master turned to the person who was being a busybody. "Touch that thing," he said.

The dreamer just looked at it. *I really would rather not touch that thing,* she thought, *but I guess I have no choice.* With great reluctance she reached out to touch it and immediately awoke from her dream.

She realized then what the Dream Master was trying to tell her. When she intruded in other people's business, some of their problems rubbed off on her. It was a very insightful dream.

The woman was given a lesson on the effect of interference from two different angles, which is often how the Dream Master gets a point across to an individual. The only purpose of these experiences on the inner planes is to make one a more spiritual being. This is why ECK is one of the best teachings on earth today. These experiences show us our weakest points and give us the insight needed to overcome them.

*These experiences show us our weakest points and give us the insight needed to overcome them.*

## A DREAM ABOUT HABITS

A woman had been running her life by the forces of power and control instead of love. Her inclination

*She realized she had developed some bad habits, but she couldn't pinpoint what they were doing to her life. So the Dream Master gave her an experience about habits.*

was to control other people, to tell them what to do. It was second nature to her. She realized she had developed some bad habits, but she couldn't pinpoint what they were doing to her life. So the Dream Master gave her an experience about habits.

One night in the dream state, the Dream Master took her into a basement with a group of people. Crust-covered leeches were crawling all over the walls and floor. The basement was dark.

The other people felt it was very important to keep plucking the leeches off themselves. They spent most of their time just sitting there, plucking and plucking.

Suddenly a door opened from the outside. Sunlight poured into the basement, and a second group of people came in. They seemed very unconcerned about these crusty creatures.

The first group tried to warn them, "Be careful of these leeches. Keep plucking them off, because they'll get all over you, and they stick! Get them off!"

The second group didn't seem to care. They were too busy laughing and enjoying themselves. The first group simply could not impress upon these happy people that leech-plucking was important enough to worry about.

The second group left the basement, and sunlight poured in through the open door. About this time, the dreamer awoke.

The dream was upsetting and left the woman with a feeling of discomfort. It showed her where she was coming up short. From this experience she developed the spiritual exercise in the previous chapter. She was able to take a bad dream one step further, to a higher level, and raise herself spiritually.

## BRIGHTER VISION

In contemplation, the woman visualized herself walking out of the dark basement into the sunlight. She made an effort to dispel the frightening effects of the dream by moving from a lower, darker world into a higher, lighter one.

As she did this, she realized that the crusty things that hung on like leeches were actually habits. They were the habits of control, fear, power, and other practices that did not allow the people she was with to have their freedom.

The second group was concerned simply with living in the love of everyday life and loving the Holy Spirit, which is the ECK. They realized that this love was in the Light and Sound, outside in the greater worlds of God.

A definite effect occurs when you begin working to change your inner space, to uplift it from power to love. Something happens out here. You begin to have brighter vision; you become more willing to allow other people as much freedom as you would like for yourself.

*You begin to have brighter vision; you become more willing to allow other people as much freedom as you would like for yourself.*

## INNER AND OUTER MASTER

Someone observed that in my talks, I was very careful to separate the Dream Master from the Outer Master. It seemed to him almost schizophrenic.

Many people not in ECK do not understand that the Inner Master and the Outer Master are really of the same origin. The same ECK current, the same flow, operates them both. I break it down for ease of understanding.

## GOLDEN NETTING

A child of four or five sometimes saw a net of gold in his inner vision. It let him see into the inner planes. The netting went up to the Soul Plane, which is the Fifth Plane, a high heaven of God. He seldom went beyond the golden netting because he simply wasn't ready for it. There was nothing there for him at that time.

Through the golden netting he sometimes saw people standing around in his backyard. Years later he would recognize them as the ECK Masters Rebazar Tarzs, Fubbi Quantz, Peddar Zaskq, and others. But at the time he thought they were just a group of people who had nothing better to do than stand around.

"Don't you guys ever do anything?" he asked them. "Don't you ever play?"

Rebazar Tarzs said to the boy, "We are here in case you need anything. We have established these forms, these shells, so that we can communicate with you. If you ever need anything, all you have to do is ask, and we are here instantly."

Though it would be many years before he found ECK, in his own way the child understood that these beings were there to be of service. They were there to pass on to him the divine love of the Sugmad, or God. If the boy had a question or needed love, they would be with him instantly.

> The child understood that these beings were there to be of service. They were there to pass on to him the divine love of the Sugmad, or God.

## ACCEPT THE GIFT

Often when the Mahanta, the Inner Master, gives these gifts of a spiritual nature, they are refused. One individual learned this lesson through her mother.

The young woman carefully shopped for a leisure suit she thought would make a great present for her mother. But when her mother opened the package and saw it, she wasn't pleased at all. "You never buy me anything I want," she said. "You always buy me what *you* want." She simply would not accept the gift.

The daughter was heartbroken. She thought the gift would be exactly what her mother wanted. She was also puzzled. Why had her mother reacted that way?

In contemplation she was given some insight into the situation. It came by way of a question from the Inner Master: How many times have you refused the gift that I have given you?

She suddenly knew why the Master often seemed sad. Again and again he gave the gift, those precious gems of truth. This truth had been presented in many different ways, in an effort to get through to the individual. Yet over and over the gift went unrecognized, and the individual turned away.

## A Higher Kind of Love

Sometime after this incident, the woman heard that a friend was in need of love and support. She intended to get in touch with him, but she kept putting it off. One night the Dream Master, Wah Z, came to her. "A friend of yours needs comfort at this time," he said. "Why don't you give him a call?"

She tried to visit him at his place of business, but his partner informed her that he hadn't come in that day. "His mother fell and broke something, and he's taking care of her."

The ECKist kept meaning to try again. She even planned to go visit her friend's mother—but she never quite got there.

One night Wah Z, Rebazar Tarzs, and Peddar Zaskq came to her in a dream. The three ECK Masters wanted to get a point across to her.

Wah Z asked, "Why didn't you visit your troubled friend?"

*Insight came by way of a question from the Inner Master: How many times have you refused the gift that I have given you?*

Rebazar Tarzs asked, "Where would you be today if I hadn't loved you when you needed me?"

Peddar Zaskq asked, "Where would you be today if I had kept the divine love inside myself and had not given it out in the works of ECK?"

The woman stood there feeling very disheartened. Then, as the ECK Masters left, Wah Z turned to her and said, "Love all things, and love the Sugmad always."

He was telling her that as we love God, we must love all things. Perhaps not in the warm, personal way in which most of us have been taught to regard love. But there is the higher kind of love, which in the Christian Bible is called charity. It is a detached love. It means to love another simply because he or she is Soul.

*Though you may find it difficult to give warm love to an individual, you can always give detached love, or charity.*

Though you may find it difficult to give warm love to an individual, you can always give detached love, or charity. This is an important principle. If you allow other people to get to you, they will pull you down from the state of spiritual awareness and happiness which is the right of every person who reaches out and accepts the gift from the Living ECK Master.

## I CAN FLY!

An ECKist had worked in the medical field for many years. One day she realized that the computer age had caught up with her. She didn't have the necessary skills to compete in today's work force. Forty years after leaving school, she realized she would have to enter the classroom again to educate herself in computer technology. She was filled with doubts about her ability to meet these new challenges.

Around that time she had a dream in which a

group of people attacked her. The interesting part was that they came after her with the tools and instruments of her profession—surgical knives and hypodermic needles.

She was terrified. She called for help from the Dream Master, but nothing seemed to happen. Suddenly a thought came to her: *I can fly! In these inner worlds, if I'm in trouble, I can fly. I'll fly higher than they can reach.*

And so she flew—above their groping hands and out of their grasp. As she sailed through the air, a woman dressed in white rose up behind her. "You can't come up here," the dreamer said. "You can't fly." The woman in white immediately fell back down to the ground.

When the dreamer awoke and thought over the dream, she saw that it was actually she who was cutting and attacking herself. She was doing it with her own attitude about her inability to learn what she needed to upgrade her skills. She was belittling herself, and in so doing, she was harming herself. It was a destructive mental action she had allowed. It would prevent her from making a better life for herself.

She recognized that the lady in white was also herself. When she said to the woman, "You can't fly," she was telling herself that she couldn't try to achieve the higher things in life. Because she had convinced one part of herself that this was true, she had condemned herself to a lower level of performance that would eventually lead to a dead end in her material life.

Soon after this, she enrolled in a class and did very well. She was surprised. But just by taking that first step, she was able to develop her self-confidence; she was creating her own worlds.

*Suddenly a thought came to her: I can fly! In these inner worlds, if I'm in trouble, I can fly.*

## WHAT YOU'RE LEARNING IN ECK

The Dream Master wants to teach you how to begin to create a better life for yourself, both here and in the inner worlds. Because, when we leave this world, we will still continue our explorations of all creation.

The inner planes are as real as the world out here. They are populated with individuals who are on missions, just as you are here. The second, third, and fourth heavens are filled with people who are still trying to find the way to God. They too are engaged in one activity or another, whether a profession or a field of art. They too are gaining experience so that they may become better and more compassionate instruments for the Holy Spirit and the Sugmad.

This life provides the experiences needed to become the very best — not in a mechanical, mental way, but spiritually. In the process, you may become very good at your profession or some other facet of life, but what you are really doing is learning to open your heart to love.

## INNER COMMUNICATION

In the Air Force I had a friend who was quite a mentalizer. We had some pretty interesting conversations during breaks at work. He liked to quote facts, but occasionally he would forget the name of something. Finally he would give up trying to remember, and we'd go back to work.

About three weeks later, he would look over at me and say the word he hadn't been able to think of before. "Thanks," I'd say and go right back to work.

It was as if the three weeks since our conversation on the subject had collapsed, and we picked up right where we had left off. He had the ability to set

*The Dream Master wants to teach you how to begin to create a better life for yourself, both here and in the inner worlds.*

up a line of inner communication between us, so that I wasn't caught off guard when he said the forgotten word out of nowhere. I always knew just what he was referring to.

This is often what happens with the Mahanta and you. Out here in the role of spiritual leader of Eckankar, I am only able to hint at the spiritual truth that exists here and in the other worlds. Part of the fault is mine, because I simply don't have the words. An equal part of the fault lies with the listener, for not having the ability to understand what is being said.

There is a link that can bridge the gap, and this is known as the inner communication of the Mahanta with the chela. When the Master speaks with the student through the inner communication, sometimes a mere phrase triggers all kinds of memories from the dream state. It can happen when you are sitting in the audience at an ECK seminar or in your own home listening to a tape of the talk. That certain phrase suddenly seems to convey a book of truth to you.

*When the Master speaks with the student through the inner communication, sometimes a mere phrase triggers all kinds of memories from the dream state.*

These are the inner teachings, the secret teachings. The insight that comes from the Golden-tongued Wisdom, whether spoken by me or someone else, is the working of the ECK, the Holy Spirit. It is trying to lift you to a higher state of consciousness.

One of the gems of truth, a golden jewel of God, has been placed in your path. When the moment occurs, look closely at the experience and weigh it carefully. Try to get all the value out of it that the Master has put into it.

## DIVINE INTERVENTION

At a past ECK seminar I talked about the principle of *deus ex machina*. It means, literally, "God from a machine," a device often used by the ancient Greek playwrights. They would place the hero in a corner he couldn't get himself out of. Not knowing exactly how to resolve the problem, the writers would contrive a *deus ex machina*. A god would descend from the sky, pick up the hero, and carry him off to safety.

The writers resorted to saving the hero by divine intervention. In a way, this device cheated the play-goer out of seeing the story resolved honestly, in terms of what is possible on the earth plane.

*ECK is all about learning to help yourself.*

The ECK teachings are not a *deus ex machina*. They are not intended to save the student from putting forth effort to get himself out of trouble.

ECK is all about learning to help yourself. Of course, if the problem gets to the point where you simply cannot help yourself, the Master can always come and help you out. But the principle behind the ECK teachings is to learn to use our own creativity to achieve a solution.

## BEAM ME UP, SCOTTY!

A Higher Initiate had a difficult time understanding this principle. He felt that his relationship with the Inner Master was such that anytime he had a bad experience, he could just say, "Wah Z, please fix this." And the problem would be magically resolved.

After the seminar the initiate had a dream. He was playing the role of Captain Kirk of the starship *Enterprise*, from the old "Star Trek" TV series. Enemy Klingons are holding him captive on a strange planet while the starship circles above.

The Living ECK Master, in the role of Scotty, is in charge of the transporter. Fans of the series know that this is a machine that beams the crew back and forth between the starship and whatever planet they are visiting.

The dreaded Klingons have taken away Captain Kirk's communicator. Luckily, he has a little electronic device hidden in his back pocket. He uses it now to signal the starship in Morse code: "Scotty, beam me up!" Over and over he sends his distress signal to the starship, but things are getting tense.

Off in the distance the dreamer sees a battered little truck, raising a dust cloud behind it as it chugs its way toward him. Behind the wheel is the Living ECK Master, playing the role of Scotty.

Scotty slams on the brakes and jumps out. He grabs Captain Kirk, pushes him in the back of the truck, and takes off driving back down the road in the direction he'd just come from.

The dreamer calls out to the Mahanta, the Living ECK Master, "Scotty, beam us up!"

"Listen," the Living ECK Master says, "I drove for thirty-five hours to get here. We're not going back the easy way!"

The dream helped the initiate to realize that he had a problem: He was being held captive by the passions of the mind. Until he could be free of them, he wouldn't get back to the starship, which symbolized the spiritual freedom to travel the worlds of God.

## HIGHER STATES OF HAPPINESS

This is an example of an inner experience that is both fun and frightening. It gives you a different insight into the other worlds. When you wake up, it stays with you for a very long time. This is one way in which the dream teachings of ECK—the most effective teachings in the world—release a person from the lower self and raise him to the higher states of happiness.

The physical world is very similar to some of the

*The dream teachings of ECK release a person from the lower self and raise him to the higher states of happiness.*

inner worlds. The same energies that flow here also flow, without interruption, into the higher planes. Even as visible light and color, these vibrations continue at higher and higher levels until they leave physical sight. But they still continue to exist at higher — and even lower — levels.

## COOKIE MASTER

A group of workers at the Eckankar Spiritual Center went out to lunch and brought some cookies back from the restaurant. One of the staff left the bag on her desk for everyone to help themselves.

In the middle of the afternoon a person from another department came to get a cookie. There were two left. He realized that a friend in his department hadn't gotten one, so he asked the staff member if he could take both cookies. "Sure," she said, handing him the bag.

His friend was on the phone when he got back to his department and didn't see him enter the room. He had other things to do, so he laid the extra cookie on her desk and went back to work. Later the friend asked him, "Did you bring me this cookie?" He was too modest to just say yes, so he fabricated a humorous story.

"Well . . . ," he said, "actually I've been writing a program to generate cookies from the computer. I finally perfected it today."

Another person, hearing the conversation, leaned over and said, "I didn't get a cookie. How does the program work?"

"Very easy," said the first man. "All you do is type C-O-O-K-I-E. He was ready to enjoy a laugh with them over his wild story when the third person, playing along with the joke, sat down at her computer and typed in the letters.

Just as she hit the return key to activate the program, another staff member rushed in the door with a cookie in her hand. "I thought someone might enjoy this," she said, and laid it on the desk of the woman who was typing.

## POWERFUL THOUGHTS

She didn't know what had just taken place, of course. By this time, not even the original storyteller knew exactly what was going on. But he realized he'd had a demonstration of the power of thought, which is another avenue of the Holy Spirit, the ECK.

The experience gave him a new respect for the words he used. It made him more consciously aware that we really do have to be careful with the thoughts we think and the words we speak.

To some people it might seem like a happy coincidence that the cookie appeared just as the computer operator hit the return key for the cookie program. But inwardly the man already knew that such things were possible. Very possibly the Dream Master had already given him an experience like this that he was unconsciously acting out in the office that very day.

In the worlds of ECK, everything fits together. Everything is in its proper time and place. When the conditions are right, when the ECK is flowing cleanly, everything works in harmony. It may not happen often, but when it does, hopefully we can recognize it as one of the golden moments of truth, a golden moment of life.

*When the conditions are right, when the ECK is flowing cleanly, everything works in harmony.*

## THE REST OF THE STORY

I have a spiritual exercise to help you deal with the occasional bad dream that leaves you feeling unsettled when you awaken. The initiate who sent this exercise in likes to listen to radio commentator Paul Harvey's "The Rest of the Story." Harvey's format provides one of the colorful spots in American radio today. He might start a story by giving a synopsis of a little-known incident in history. Then he breaks for a commercial. When he comes back, he says, "And now, here's the rest of the story," and continues in more detail.

In one instance, he told a story about a certain man's life, beginning from childhood. You didn't know who he was talking about at first. He described how, as a child, the person was very slow in school. "Your son is retarded," his parents were told by the teacher. "He belongs in a special school." But his mother felt the teacher was wrong. Her son had an interest in mathematics and science, fields that his teacher never suspected the boy knew anything about.

After Paul Harvey had recounted all these little details about the individual, he ended the story by saying, "And that was the life of Albert Einstein." He has a way of making history more interesting.

The ECKist decided to adapt a similar format to help her work out disturbing dreams. She started with the assumption that there was a gap in her dreams, a part of the story the censor had not allowed to come through.

*This is a four-step spiritual exercise, and the steps are very easy.*

This is a four-step spiritual exercise, and the steps are very easy. Starting with the assumption that you do not know everything that happened in the dream, the first step is to go into contemplation. Visualize turning on the radio, and listen for the Sound in the form of the narrator's voice.

Second, listen to the narrator relating the details of your dream up to the time you awakened. Imagine that he is giving you a synopsis of your dream.

Third, take a commercial break, and while it's going on, chant HU. At some point, the voice returns and says, "And now, here's the rest of your dream."

Finally, imagine the voice of the narrator taking your dream to the next step.

*ECK Worldwide Seminar, Atlanta, Georgia,*
*Saturday, October 22, 1988*

The struggle of the emperor moth is essentially the struggle of Soul in the lower worlds.

# 3

# THE STRUGGLE OF AN EMPEROR MOTH

*T*he struggle of the emperor moth is essentially the struggle of Soul in the lower worlds. It is an important phase of Soul's development. Through our experiences here on earth, Soul develops the beauty and grace It needs to become a Co-worker with God. And when the time is right, the individual is led to the path of ECK, to begin the most direct journey to God.

## PEN PALS

An ECK initiate began to correspond with a pen pal some twenty years ago, when she was a horse-crazy seventh grader. The other girl, whose name she had gotten from a magazine on horses, shared the same interest. They wrote back and forth for many years about one thing or another, but they never met.

Even after the initiate joined Eckankar, she stayed away from any mention of it in her letters. She didn't know how her pen pal would feel about a new-age religious teaching.

She was pleasantly surprised when her friend wrote and said that she had been reading about some of the new-age religions and found them very intriguing. The initiate could hardly wait to write back and ask, "Have you ever heard about Eckankar?"

The pen pal began asking hard questions about Eckankar. She also shared some of her own experiences, which were eye-openers even to the ECKist. Each person's experiences are different from those of others. There may be similarities, but essentially your own experiences are as unique as you are.

*Just as the moth must wait for the proper time to come out of the cocoon, the ECK sets the stage for you to come into Eckankar.*

Some twenty years after their first contact, the pen pal became a student of ECK. Today, after many years of corresponding and dealing with life's struggles, both women look back and realize what has taken place. They now see that even when they were seventh graders, the ECK had already taken a hand in seeing that they came to the teachings of ECK.

Just as the moth must wait for the proper time to come out of the cocoon, the ECK sets the stage for you to come into Eckankar. The same applies to those you will reach as a missionary of ECK. The way has been prepared, but you have to go forth and make the effort.

## MISSIONARY OF ECK

When I mentioned we were missionaries in ECK, someone said, "This is the first time you've ever used the word *missionary*. It could be quite a shock to some of the ECKists."

"But I have a mission," I explained, "and the person who carries out a mission is a missionary. In fact, every single ECKist is on a mission and has been from the day they came into Eckankar."

"But they don't all think of it like that," the initiate said. "Most people associate the word *missionary* with Christianity."

He had a point, of course, so I would like to explain

the difference between an ECK missionary and the stereotypical Christian missionary.

A Christian missionary has a message he feels is worthwhile to give to the world. Yet, he may not always be as ready to recognize the beauty of God's creation in another belief or teaching. He may overlook the possibility that a teaching which has existed for centuries might have something worthwhile in it.

We in ECK must be willing to let other people have their own beliefs. It would be totally useless to present ECK with the attitude: I know it all, ours is the best, and no matter what you say, I'm going to outtalk you until I convince you, in whatever way it takes, that you should follow my path.

This attitude was once part of the Christian missionary efforts among the Native Americans, Africans, the Sandwich Islanders (native Hawaiians), and in many other parts of the world. History has shown that once Christianity got the upper hand, those who did not wish to give up their "heathen" religions were persecuted.

*An ECK missionary will learn at least as much as he or she has to teach.*

An ECK missionary will learn at least as much as he or she has to teach. If we keep this in mind, we will keep the humility needed to stay in balance as we present the ECK teachings to the rest of the world.

## HUMILITY

Someone asked me, "Could you give a spiritual exercise to bring humility?" I gave his question a lot of thought. I figured if I stretched my own imagination and creativity, surely I could come up with an exercise in how to reach humility.

But I just couldn't do it. How can a spiritual exercise be geared to help another person achieve humility?

*The Spiritual Exercises of ECK accomplish numerous purifications in the spiritual body.*

The Spiritual Exercises of ECK accomplish numerous purifications in the spiritual body. It is through this process that one also gains humility. You might keep in mind what I just said: As a missionary of ECK, you have as much to learn as you have to teach. If there were a spiritual exercise for humility, this would be it.

## OPPOSITE PAGES

An ECK couple had been together for several years. One day the man looked at his mate and said, "We are so totally different. I wonder why we're still together after all this time?" The woman had often wondered about the same thing. They had nothing in common, not even their general outlook on life.

One day the man received his monthly discourse from the Eckankar Spiritual Center. It was discourse number six of the *Soul Travel 1* series. When he opened it up, he found that half the pages were blank. Still, he began to read every other page, trying to figure out what the missing pages were about. But he couldn't make the connection.

He called the Eckankar Spiritual Center to ask what had happened. "It was just a printing error," he was told. "We'll send you another discourse."

Before the man's replacement discourse arrived, his mate received her monthly mailing from Eckankar. She was taking the same discourse as he—*Soul Travel 1*, number six. "I'll just read yours until mine arrives," he said. When she opened her discourse, she found that half of the pages were blank too. But the printed pages in her discourse were exactly the ones that were missing in his.

As a former printer, I would say the odds of that happening are pretty incredible.

The man had wondered how such opposites could stay together, and the answer came through the ECK discourses. He realized that his and her attributes together were teaching them lessons they could not hope to learn alone — about the spiritual path, about life and living, and about love. Although they were quite opposite in their ways, together they formed a more complete unit.

## PLUM CAKE

The Dream Master works in your life to give you spiritual understanding about things that might otherwise be passed over. Without this understanding, you would kick aside the gems of truth and walk right by them. You would never see what the Holy Spirit places in your path every day, often ankle-deep.

An ECK initiate in Austria had a dream that told her to go to Corsica, France. There she would find opportunities for work and training in certain areas. She and several friends made plans to take the trip together.

The day they arrived in France, the group went to a restaurant quite a distance from their hotel. It was clean and pleasant, but the ECKist found the food very different from what she was used to at home. Over their meal they made plans for the next day. Everyone agreed they should try out different restaurants during their stay in France.

That night the ECKist had another dream. In it she and a few friends were having the same discussion they'd had while she was awake—where would they eat tomorrow. One of her friends said, "The restaurant where we ate today is a good place, and they might even have plum cake." This was a favorite of the dreamer.

*The Dream Master works in your life to give you spiritual understanding about things that might otherwise be passed over.*

The next morning the group talked it over again. "Let's eat at the same place as yesterday," the ECKist suggested. "It's clean, and maybe I can get some plum cake there." One of her friends pointed out that plums are a rarity in that area of France. "And anyway," he added, "it's too dull. The rest of us would rather try a different place today."

The group split up and went their separate ways. When the ECKist and a companion arrived at the restaurant, she saw something in the dessert display case that looked like a plum cake, the kind that's usually found in Austria. The waiter confirmed it. "Yes indeed, it's plum cake," he said. "It's the first time we've had it in weeks." He called it by a certain name in French. The word he used was similar to what it was called in her own language. All of this reinforced the validity of her dream.

She also realized that the Dream Master hadn't led her to that restaurant just for plum cake. The dream was an indicator of where she could safely eat during her stay in France. This was always a matter of concern to her when she traveled. She had a sensitivity to certain foods and tried to stay away from those that were harmful to her health. The dream had provided the help she needed while away from home.

An interesting aside is that some of the friends who went to another restaurant became ill from food poisoning. The illness recurred throughout their stay as they continued to experiment with different places. The ECKist and her companion returned to the original restaurant every day for the rest of their stay.

## SPIRITUAL FREEDOM

A Fourth Initiate in ECK became ill. After a physical examination, his doctor informed him that he would need triple-bypass surgery. "I don't understand how you've managed to live this long without the operation," the doctor said.

The ECKist was admitted into the hospital and assigned a room. As he and his wife were chatting, a young social worker poked her head in the door. "May I come in and talk with you for a while?" she asked. "Sure," he said.

She wanted to know if he had any fears about the operation that was to be performed the following day.

"No, I'm not particularly scared," the ECKist said.

The social worker was taken aback. She was used to people being scared out of their wits by this type of surgery. Scanning his file, she said, "I notice you list your religious preference as Eckankar. I've never heard of that before."

The man told her a little about Eckankar. He said, "I've learned that Soul is the eternal part of each of us. I am Soul, and I happen to be in this physical body for this lifetime to get certain experiences." She asked him several questions, and he tried his best to answer. Before she left, she said, "I came here to help you, but I think you've helped me."

The next day, as the ECKist regained consciousness after the surgery, he remembered being in a beautiful place with the Inner Master, the Dream Master. He had waved good-bye to the Mahanta just as he came back to his physical body in the recovery room. He was then moved to another room with three beds. One of his roommates was an eighty-one-year-old man, and the other was a younger Christian man.

"Don't worry about getting your strength back," the younger man said. "God is with us."

Over the next few days, the three men formed a friendship. They passed the time discussing the

*"I've learned that Soul is the eternal part of each of us. I am Soul, and I happen to be in this physical body for this lifetime to get certain experiences."*

different aspects of life. The two other patients were intrigued with some of the subjects the ECKist brought up—karma, reincarnation, past lives, Soul, and spiritual freedom.

One day a voice from the door said, "Can I come in?" It was the social worker who had greeted the ECKist the day he was admitted. "I overheard some of your conversation," she said, "and if you don't mind, I'd like to hear more."

The social worker and the three roommates continued the discussion, which by now was primarily about Eckankar. As they talked, the ECKist realized that he had been pretty smug about his knowledge of ECK before coming to the hospital. He had gained a lot of intellectual knowledge up to that point, but he still hadn't experienced the learning of the heart. But as he attempted to answer his two roommates' questions over the last few days, he found he was learning even more about ECK than he had in all the years he had been studying it.

"I like what you're saying about spiritual freedom," the social worker said. "The Christian church I belong to has a long list of dos and don'ts. I'm not sure why."

The ECKist said, "The orthodox churches are there to give you the strength to get through your everyday life, until you develop the necessary spiritual strength to be ready for Eckankar."

What he was saying was that there is a place for the other religions; otherwise God would not have created them. If we feel ours is the only path, we overlook the fact that God created the rest of the religions for a reason: because Soul needs them. And when we in ECK forget this, we become as vain as the missionaries of the other religions.

*If we feel ours is the only path, we overlook the fact that God created the rest of the religions for a reason: because Soul needs them.*

Finally the ECKist was released from the hospital. A day or two after he got home, the phone rang. He was too weak to take the call, so his wife answered. It was someone from the Spiritual Services department at the ECK Spiritual Center, just wanting to know how he felt. His wife told the caller that the operation had gone quite well.

In the next day's mail, he received a pink slip for his Fifth Initiation. A glance at the postmark revealed that it had been mailed the same day he was released from the hospital, a day or two before the call from the ECK Spiritual Center.

## FORWARD PROGRESS IN ECK

As most ECKists know, the stretch between initiations can be a long, long process. The man found it interesting that these major incidents—his surgery followed by receiving the pink slip—seemed tied together. During his stay in the hospital, he had undergone a change.

In the Fourth Initiation, one's understanding of ECK is often predominately intellectual. It is hoped that, by the time one reaches the Fifth Initiation, the mind has lost its hold on the all-seeing vision of Soul. At this point, one ought to operate more from love and with the heart. This is not always the case, of course. As we move through our initiations, it is not necessarily steady, forward progress.

*As we move through our initiations, it is not necessarily steady, forward progress.*

## OUT OF THE COCOON

There are times when you move straight forward in understanding. There are also times when you move in an elliptical orbit; you swing back for a while, but when you eventually swing forward again, you go further than you had been before. So after a certain

All too often we take for granted the gifts of the Mahanta. We forget to appreciate the gift of finding the ECK teachings in this lifetime.

period of time spent in this back-and-forth motion in the form of an elliptical circle, you become established in, say, the Fourth Plane. Then you are ready to go on to the next level of initiation.

All too often we take for granted the gifts of the Mahanta. We forget to appreciate the gift of finding the ECK teachings in this lifetime. Instead, we complain about our struggles as we work our way out of our cocoon, without realizing that they are necessary to reach the sublime beauty of Soul.

## "YOU KNOW HIM"

An ECKist went to see a friend who had just had a baby the month before. Her friend was not in Eckankar. During their visit, the ECKist noticed that tears were running down the cheeks of the baby. "She cries all the time," the mother explained. "I can't seem to make her stop."

"Why don't we sing HU?" the ECKist suggested. She didn't explain that it is a love song to God; she just said, "HU is a healing sound, and maybe it will help."

She began to sing HU, and her friend joined in. Pretty soon they noticed that the baby had stopped crying. In fact, she even tried to smile for the first time.

Later, as the ECK initiate was driving home in her car, the Soul in the infant's body came to her and said, "You know him." The woman was caught off guard. "Who do you mean?" she asked. The Soul who was the baby replied, "The Mahanta, the Living ECK Master. You know him."

As Soul, the child had come from a beautiful place. But then she entered the Physical Plane, which is relatively dark compared to the worlds that exist on the Astral, Causal, Mental, and higher planes. Up to that day, the child had feared that she had lost contact with the Mahanta, the Living ECK Master whom she had met on the other planes.

After that, whenever the ECKist visited her friend and found the baby crying, all she had to do was pick her up. Immediately the infant would nestle against her and fall asleep.

One reason we take the gift of the ECK teachings for granted is because we have forgotten the separation from the Sound and Light. In the human consciousness, we forget that there ever was a connection. And because we do not remember, we don't always appreciate the gift of the Master when it is put in front of us. But the baby remembered.

## THE STRUGGLE OF AN EMPEROR MOTH

A biologist found the cocoon of an emperor moth and took it to his lab for study. *What a wonderful opportunity to watch it come out and unfold into a slender creature with beautiful wings,* he thought. It sat on his lab table for quite a while. Finally the cocoon began to tremble as the moth made its efforts to come out into the world.

The scientist noticed that the cocoon was shaped like a bottle, wide at the bottom but very narrow at the top. The top was surrounded by a concretelike substance. The scientist thought there was no way the moth would make it through that hard material.

He watched the cocoon for a while, growing more and more impatient. Finally he decided to help the moth out. He would make it a little easier for the moth to get into the world. Using a tiny pair of scissors, he carefully cut through the concretelike rim at the top of the cocoon. The moth popped out almost instantly.

The biologist waited for the moth to spread its

*One reason we take the gift of the ECK teachings for granted is because we have forgotten the separation from the Sound and Light.*

beautiful wings and show its pretty colors. But nothing happened. The moth was misshapen, with a huge body and very tiny wings. He watched it walk around slowly, unable to lift itself off the table. Eventually it died, never having flown.

The scientist began to read about the emperor moth, trying to figure out what had happened. He found that other biologists had made the same mistake he had. They too had tried to ease the moth's difficult entry into the world by cutting the lip of the cocoon. But they had discovered the purpose for the cocoon being wide at the bottom with a narrow neck and a very tight top.

As the moth forces itself through the narrow neck of the cocoon, it must streamline its body. The fluids in its body are squeezed into the wings. This process makes the wings large and the body small. When it finally emerges into the world, the emperor moth is a creature unsurpassed in beauty.

The biologist realized that he had actually done the moth a disservice by sparing it what he considered unnecessary hardship. Deprived of its natural birthing process, the moth had emerged a misshapen creature, incapable of fulfilling its potential.

It might seem like an apparent contradiction that the emperor moth must go through such a slow, intense struggle to get out of its cocoon in order to be born into the world as a beautiful creature.

Quite often the ECKists approach the Mahanta, the Living ECK Master to complain about the hardships in their life. "Why is my life so difficult?" they'll ask. "Why can't you take this burden away from me?" The problems they cite generally fall under three major categories: health, finances, and love life. If the problem isn't resolved quickly enough for them, they'll

*The biologist realized he had done the moth a disservice by sparing it what he considered unnecessary hardship.*

ask, "Haven't you any power?"

They don't realize that an intervention at the wrong time, or too soon, can create a misshapen form not properly prepared to reach the high worlds of God, the Sugmad.

## TOTAL FREEDOM AND TOTAL RESPONSIBILITY

We often do to our own children what the biologist did to the moth. After all, we want them to have every advantage. We pile money upon them. We make sure they get to attend all the proper social occasions.

Children today are no different than they were in my generation. The only difference is that we survived and became adults. Now that we have children of our own, we forget that we said the same things to our parents that our children are saying now: "Please let me go here, let me go there, everybody else is doing it," and so on.

This puts a lot of pressure on parents. We love our children, just as our parents loved us. But with misguided tenderness, we sometimes give in too quickly and just say yes. This can be a disservice to our children. It doesn't allow them to develop in a correct spiritual way.

*We love our children, just as our parents loved us. But with misguided tenderness, we sometimes give in too quickly and just say yes.*

This attitude was common in the earlier days of Eckankar. The parents were still in the flower-child years of their own youth, and they didn't want to restrict their children's freedom in any way. But it was freedom without responsibility.

This principle was often overlooked by parents in the early days of ECK. They became very upset when other people tried to set their children straight by saying, "Hey, quit kicking my shins." Anyone who corrected their children was interfering with their total freedom. The parents were unbalanced in that they didn't yet realize that with total freedom comes total responsibility.

## WHAT DO I HAVE TO LEARN?

*The Law of Life provides the way to higher consciousness as surely as the moth is given a way out of the cocoon.*

The Mahanta, the Living ECK Master realizes even when the chela is kicking and struggling in the cocoon of his own troubles that this struggle is good for him. The individual can work out of it, if he will just keep trying. The Law of Life provides the way to higher consciousness as surely as the moth is given a way out of the cocoon.

You must always remember this. When hardships come, don't automatically ask God to deliver you from them. Perhaps it would be wiser to ask: What do I have to learn before I am delivered from this problem? Then direct your attention and creativity toward the spiritual lesson to be learned as you try to get out of your cocoon. In doing this, you develop the sublime beauty of Soul.

## ALWAYS WITH YOU

Someone mentioned the other night that I hadn't ended the talk with the ancient blessing of the Vairagi Order — "May the blessings be," or "Baraka Bashad." They said it felt like the talk wasn't complete. Whether I say it or not, keep in mind that the presence of the Master is always with you. The blessing is always with you; the gift of the Master is always with you. It is a gift just waiting to be received.

I would like you to remember that I am always with you, on your journey home and on your journey into the worlds of God. May the blessings be.

*ECK Worldwide Seminar, Atlanta, Georgia,*
*Sunday, October 23, 1988*

You are on your own path to God. There isn't any hurry. If you think in terms of being slower or faster than someone else, then you are in a race. That is not the path to God.

# 4

# COULD I PLEASE PAY FOR THAT HONEY? PART 1

On the flight to Australia, a young woman was seated next to my wife and me. We are generally pretty quiet when we travel. We may chat a little bit, but usually I use the time to write or sometimes read a mystery novel, which I find very relaxing.

During the flight the young woman reached into her luggage and pulled out a notebook, then spent the next several hours filling page after page with notes. *How can such a young person have so much to write about?* I wondered. She hadn't lived long enough to have that many experiences. I wanted to ask her about it, but she was so busy that I didn't want to disturb her.

Finally, as the plane was landing in Sydney, I leaned over and whispered to my wife, "I have to ask her what she's writing. If I don't, I'll wonder about it for the rest of my life."

It turned out she was a college student from Melbourne. "I've spent the last four months traveling through North America," she said. "I really enjoyed it, but it was time to come home." She told us about some of her adventures as she traveled through Canada to the United States and Mexico, staying in youth hostels. "Except in Mexico," she added. "In Mexico I was able to live very economically without them."

She said, "The four months passed very quickly; a lot of things happened. I want to write down my experiences while the images are fresh in my mind." Someday, she figured, if she decided to write more about them, she would be able to refer to her notebook to recapture the past.

## DREAM JOURNAL

*If these inner experiences are not recorded when they happen, most of them will be forgotten.*

This is one of the reasons I recommend that ECK initiates keep a dream journal. If these inner experiences are not recorded when they happen, most of them will be forgotten. Even if an experience doesn't seem to mean much now, at some point in the future you might look back at it and recognize its spiritual significance.

Not every dream will predict the future or give some insight into the individual's life. Dreams are another face of reality in the same way that our everyday life is another face of reality. For some people, their waking life is just part of the dream. Their dreams, visions, and inner experiences are so real that they don't separate them from everyday life. They are able to integrate and weave their inner and outer lives into one whole unit of spiritual existence.

## MAKING SENSE

I recently got a letter from an ECKist who had two questions about dreams. He has a marvelous way of phrasing his questions. The first one was: "Why have only a small number of my clear and meaningful dreams come true, while the rest read like beautiful, fanciful stories full of empty expectations?"

If Soul were operating from the highest state possible, seeing with a 360-degree viewpoint, then everything that happened in Its physical and inner worlds would make sense. But when It sees from a limited viewpoint, certain things don't seem logical. Therefore they don't make sense.

Traditionally, religion has been taught in such a way that life and our relationship with divinity is actually mentalized. If someone has an experience that we don't understand, we say, "That doesn't make sense," which translates to, "It's not valid." Our own inability to see the logic is used to discredit someone else's belief.

## WHY DO DREAMS FADE?

The second question the man asked about dreams was: "If dreams are designed by God and his spiritual agents to warn, encourage, inspire, and reveal important information to an individual, why do most dreams fade away so fast upon a person's wakening? Why are other dreams so vague and fleeting that the dreamer does not even know that he or she has had a dream or dreams?"

*Like an early spring flower, some people unfold sooner than others. Why? It's the individuality of Soul.*

If you examine it with logic, the fact that some dreams fade away makes them seem almost like a wasted effort. What good are they? But here again, it's a matter of consciousness, not logic.

Like an early spring flower, some people unfold sooner than others. Why? It's the individuality of Soul, the difference between each of us. Soul picks Its own path to God, in Its own time, in Its own way. To put it another way, some people have to work a little harder to extract the honey from the honeycomb.

## SOUL IS UNIQUE

There are a number of recognized religions in the world. But in truth, there are as many religions in the world as there are people. Soul is unique, an individual being. No two Souls are alike. No two people have exactly the same experiences. Therefore, no two people have exactly the same outlook on life.

## A RELIGION THAT RESPONDS TO SOUL

Those with similar outlooks often come together in loosely or tightly knit groups. These are labeled religions. Within each religious group is a central core of people who follow its teachings from cradle to grave. Others, travelers on the boundaries of the established beliefs, are just passing through. They haven't found the teaching that responds to their own spiritual needs.

How do they know that a religion doesn't respond? They aren't always able to put it into words because their reasons may not seem logical. Yet they know they are not satisfied with what they have.

## EXPLORING

People sometimes stay with the religion of their youth just because getting out is too uncomfortable. If all of your relatives are members of a certain faith, it's more or less expected of you to do the same. It just wouldn't do for you to suddenly change religions; you would be made to feel that you had destroyed the social structure of your family. This is strong pressure. It keeps many people from seeking truth.

Those in less rigid family groups are able to explore. One family member tries this, another tries that, another tries nothing at all, and they all get along. But families with a very rigid structure can impose strong rules to dictate what each member must believe and how he must conduct himself in order not to be ostracized. And in the midst of all these settings, we try to find our way in life.

## Getting a Glass of Water

A principle in good storytelling is to establish a goal at the beginning of the story, then have the main character go through a struggle to reach it. As an example, let's suppose the main character is me. I'm onstage giving a talk. Suddenly I get very thirsty, and my goal is to drink some water. If all I have to do is pick up the glass of water conveniently placed on the table next to me, we have no story.

So let's make the struggle more challenging. I'm giving a talk, I'm very thirsty, and my goal is to drink some water. I reach for the glass that's usually placed on the table next to me, but it's not there. Someone forgot to put it there when the stage was being set up.

"I'm really thirsty," I mention to the audience.

"There's some water at the back of the auditorium," someone yells. "You're welcome to it." My throat is too dry to continue without something to drink. But I figure I can keep talking while I walk to the back of the hall to get a glass of water.

I leave the stage and take about ten steps up the aisle. The microphone jerks out of my hand. I hadn't realized the cord was so short. Now I've got another problem: If I want the water, I have to stop the talk long enough to go to the back of the hall and return to the stage. But I'm really thirsty, so I leave the microphone and head for the water.

As I walk up the aisle, someone from the audience comes up and says, "I'd like to ask you a question.

You're handy right now, so I think this is as good a time as any."

Now there are two obstacles between me and the water: the person trying to ask his question as we walk, and the audience sitting around waiting for me to come back.

I start walking faster because I want to get my water and get back onstage—and my shoe comes off. I don't want anyone to know, and I certainly don't want to walk all the way to back of the room with my shoe off. But I can't get it on without bending down and using both hands, which I don't want to do. Third problem.

Farther along, I trip over a chair and fall. Someone reaches out to help me up and accidentally pulls my jacket off. By the time I finally make it to the back of the room and take a drink, I think to myself, *This is the best glass of water I have ever tasted. It has a completely different flavor than if it had been sitting handily on the table beside me.* The difference is in the experience I gained in the struggle to reach my goal. This is what our life is about—experience.

## SUBJECTIVE AND OBJECTIVE EXPERIENCE

*Soul came from the high spiritual planes into the lower worlds.*

Soul came from the high spiritual planes into the lower worlds. The lower worlds include the Physical Plane as well as the Astral, Causal, Mental, and Etheric Planes. The Astral Plane is the plane of emotions on the subjective side. On the objective side, certain parts of it are known as the area of ghosts, flying saucers, and things of this nature.

The subjective side of the Causal Plane is memory. It is an area of your mind that retains all the events of the past.

Beyond this is the Mental Plane, the area of the

mind that works in the present. Unlike the remembering faculty, this is the active area that you work from to make plans, analyze, and solve problems as they arise in the present time.

## BEING SHOWN THE PAST

Then comes the Etheric Plane, which is the unconscious, or subconscious, area. It is the high part of the mind that houses unconscious attitudes, some of which were acquired through karmic experiences in past lives. This often accounts for why we have certain talents or why we are instinctively drawn to one person and repelled by another.

At a certain stage in our spiritual unfoldment we may be shown, through dreams or Soul Travel, a past-life experience that explains a present love, hate, or fear. There is a particular reason, for instance, why some people have a fear of heights. Fear has many faces. Each face has a specialized reason. Usually—though not always—it is based on something that happened in a past life.

*At a certain stage in our spiritual unfoldment we may be shown, through dreams or Soul Travel, a past-life experience that explains a present love, hate, or fear.*

## OPEN SLOWLY

The Spiritual Exercises of ECK are a self-discipline. If you are interested in doing them, you begin to open yourself to the eternal wisdom, the divine consciousness that you are. This is a first step.

It would not be wise, at any time, to open up instantly to the high awareness of God Consciousness. Whether an individual believes it or not, the shock would be too much.

Sometimes we have problems with even little changes. When we travel to another country, for instance, certain customs or phrases can cause a real cultural shock. Places where the light switch has to

*The Spiritual Exercises of ECK are a self-discipline.*

be pushed down to turn a light on, instead of up as we are accustomed to doing in the United States, can be confusing at first. An Australian visiting in America would be in for an interesting experience if he asked for a lift. Americans, who don't know it as an elevator, would have no idea what he meant.

The point is, if one were to open up to God all at once, the experience would be shattering.

## ECK TERMINOLOGY

We in ECK have a trinity, if you will, and it goes like this.

First there is the Sugmad, which is our term for God. Then there is the ECK, the Voice of God, more commonly known as the Holy Spirit or Divine Spirit, and sometimes referred to as the Holy Ghost, Divine Comforter, Paraclete, and so on.

*The ECK, the Voice of God, is heard as Sound and seen as Light.*

The ECK has two aspects, and these are the mainstay of the teachings. They are known as Sound and Light. The ECK, the Voice of God, is heard as Sound and seen as Light.

## WHAT IS THE MAHANTA?

Then we have the Mahanta. The best way to explain the Mahanta is as a personalized version of the Sound and Light. He works as the Outer and the Inner Master. He brings the message of ECK to the outer world through the written and spoken word. He also works with people inwardly in the dream state, during Soul Travel, and in other ways.

It is a bit difficult to explain the Mahanta to people who are not familiar with the Eckankar teachings. This is why we put so much stock in experience. ECK is the path of experience. Once you have the experience, then you have a reason to believe and, if you choose, to go forward in the life of ECK. But

I don't ask you to go forward; that's up to you.

To give a more specific definition, the Mahanta is the Inner Master and the Living ECK Master is the Outer Master. The Mahanta, the Living ECK Master also operates on each of the inner planes. On the Astral Plane, for instance, he has a body which corresponds to the properties of that plane. Therefore, he is as real to those who live on the Astral Plane as he is to those who live here on the Physical Plane.

But even there, as on every plane in the lower worlds, there is the inner, unseen part which is the Mahanta. On every plane in the lower worlds, the Mahanta, the Living ECK Master works and operates to lift Soul to Its heritage of God Consciousness.

*On every plane in the lower worlds, the Mahanta, the Living ECK Master works and operates to lift Soul to Its heritage of God Consciousness.*

## THE TWO GARDENERS

Early yesterday morning I looked out the window of my hotel room. Out by the roadside were two gardeners, each holding a shovel. They were standing near a row of twelve little trees that were planted alongside the road.

They began to dig up the ground around one of the trees, occasionally stopping to tug it to the left, the right, then back to the left. *Is the tree growing crookedly?* I wondered. I hoped they weren't trying to straighten it that way. If you try to straighten a crooked tree all at once, it will only break off. The best way is to tie a cable around it, secure the cable to the ground, and let the tree have a season or so to grow in the new direction.

Watching them from my hotel-room window gave me a strange feeling. Everything looked so small — tiny people, tiny cars and trucks, tiny trees. It was like peering through a glass wall at a giant, well-organized ant farm where everything ran smoothly. Except for the two men tugging on that little tree.

Ten or fifteen minutes later, they pulled it out of the ground and threw it aside. *Thank goodness,* I thought, *they've finished their job and can leave now.* Instead, they walked a little farther along to the second tree. They must have sweated and toiled for a full twenty minutes, digging with their shovels and tugging the tree back and forth, before they managed to pull that little thing out of the ground.

Then the two men flopped to the ground and took a rest, probably planning their attack on the next tree. I wondered why they hadn't brought along some kind of machinery to make their job easier.

I stopped watching and did some work for a few hours, and then my wife and I went out to lunch. When we got back to the room, I remembered the two gardeners. I glanced out the window to check their progress.

Ten trees had been removed. One tree way at the far end was very green, so they had left it. The second remaining tree didn't look too healthy, but I was quite a distance away. Maybe they left it because it still had a green leaf or two. I said to my wife, "The twelve trees were probably planted last season, and they got one good one out of twelve, possibly two." I still thought the second one was doubtful.

It reminded me of the people who come to the spiritual path of ECK, looking for truth. They stay for a season, and then there seems to be a drought. Ten out of twelve may feel they didn't get the water they needed. But since one person did, and possibly two, it is a climate in which some can thrive.

> The two gardeners had a task similar to the one that faces the Mahanta, the Living ECK Master.

## YOUR SPIRITUAL SEASON

The two gardeners had a task similar to the one that faces the Mahanta, the Living ECK Master.

Like the twelve trees, the people who come to the Living ECK Master all want a chance to bloom and grow. But for some trees, the climate is not right. They get too much sun and they dry out.

A season later the gardeners come along and say, "These ten didn't work out. This one is borderline. We'll give it extra care—a little extra love, more water, fertilizer, hugs—whatever it takes to make the tree grow right." There is also the other tree— the one out of twelve that flourished and grew.

Every season there are those who come to ECK, stay for a while, then say, in effect, "It's not for me; it's not my time yet, it's not my season." Others are still weighing things. For one reason or another, they can't decide whether they should stay and thrive, or wait for another season.

*Soul cannot be lost; therefore, It cannot be saved. But It can be liberated.*

People tend to project their own religious beliefs onto Eckankar, so I want to make this clear: Comparing people with the ten trees that died is not meant to imply that those who don't thrive in Eckankar are spiritually dead or lost. This is not true. Soul cannot be lost; therefore, It cannot be saved. But It can be liberated.

## BREAKING FREE

In a way, the lower worlds are a prison, walled up by time, space, matter, and energy, from which Soul has to break free. Once It had the opportunity to have the knowledge of God—like the glass of water close at hand—but It did not appreciate the gift. So God sent Soul into the lower worlds for experience.

The experience is not always pleasant, and some people tend to personalize the obstacles that confront Soul. In ECK we refer to the negative force, and as a matter of convenience we call it the Kal force. In

Christianity the negative force is generally known as Satan or the devil. Many people never gain a real understanding of why God would allow Satan to exist if God were so much more powerful. All they know is, when anything goes wrong, lay it on Satan.

A woman who had been divorced for a few years received a letter from her ex-husband. "God brought us together," he wrote, "but Satan tore us apart."

That didn't sit too well with the woman. "That spineless, no-good bum doesn't have enough backbone to take responsibility for the breakup," she said. "Now he's trying to pin it on that poor devil, Satan." I thought that was an interesting response.

A person who doesn't understand the negative force thinks of it as evil. "Why doesn't God just step on Satan and squash him?" he'll ask. "That would take care of the problem, and we could all live happily ever after."

If we could walk through life without any obstacles, Soul would learn absolutely nothing. The obstacles that occur along the way are to give Soul experience; they are responsible for the purification and maturity of Soul. The experiences are necessary for Soul to become a Co-worker with God. This is Its final purpose.

## ECK-VIDYA

*Sometimes the Master works with people through the ECK-Vidya.*

Sometimes the Master works with people through the ECK-Vidya. It is known as the ancient science of prophecy, but this is a very narrow definition. In a real sense, the ECK-Vidya takes in the past, present, and future. It looks to the future if there is a real need for Soul to know something.

Knowledge of the ECK-Vidya may come through the dream state, in contemplation, through Soul

Travel, or sometimes by direct knowing. There are a number of different ways for an individual to get this experience.

Another way in which the ECK-Vidya comes is through the Golden-tongued Wisdom. This is when the ECK, the Holy Spirit, speaks to you through the voice of another person. I am not talking about mediumship here; that is a very low form of spiritual unfoldment, regardless of what many people think.

## STAYING IN THE DRIVER'S SEAT

I read an article about a man who acts as a channel for a being who calls himself Lazaris. The medium normally wears glasses and is a very nice-looking person. As Lazaris takes over and begins to speak through him, he takes his glasses off. There was a photograph of him with his glasses off and his eyes shut as he was being interviewed.

I have to question why anyone would get out of the driver's seat and go unconscious. It's like letting someone else take the car out with your driver's license and credit cards. People who allow themselves to be channels for spirits from the other side are doing just that. Furthermore, they are stunting their own spiritual growth. They may be learning something, but not about Soul's greatest aspect, which is creativity.

*Soul works in high awareness, not no awareness.*

Soul works in high awareness, not no awareness. When you go unconscious and let someone speak their message through you, you are not in a state of awareness. Where is the awareness if you later have to listen to the message on tape like everyone else, or read the notes that someone took and hope they got it right? Yet often the people hearing the message will assume it is truth. Why? For no practical reason

*These are all stages in Soul's progression toward the high worlds of God.*

except that it's a little strange, this man speaking in a different voice with his eyes shut.

I can't say across the board that no one is helped by a person like this, because some people are helped. These are all stages in Soul's progression toward the high worlds of God. But mediumship is not a very high level at all in Soul's journey into the spiritual planes.

## FORTUNE COOKIE

This next story is one example of how the ECK speaks to an individual through the Golden-tongued Wisdom.

An ECKist went out to lunch with a friend. As they ate, his friend told him a joke about a fat couple who sat in a booth next to him in another restaurant. The ECKist, thinking that was really a funny story, filed it away in his head for retelling at a later date.

The next evening he met a business associate for dinner at a Chinese restaurant. They finished their meal and asked for the check, which the waitress placed on the table along with two fortune cookies. As the ECKist picked up his fortune cookie, a large couple came in and took the next booth. Reminded of his friend's story, he wondered if this might be the same couple. The thought struck him funny.

*In ECK we learn to keep our spiritual eyes and ears open.*

He broke open his cookie, then leaned over and began to whisper the story to his associate. He unfolded the little piece of paper as he talked. He glanced down to read it. The message from the fortune cookie said: "When one speaks only good about others, there is no need to whisper." The ECKist stopped the story in midsentence.

In ECK we learn to keep our spiritual eyes and ears open. As soon as he saw what was on the paper, he knew that the ECK, the Mahanta, was giving him a very direct message. He also knew that it was for his own good.

"Go on with the story," the other man said. "I want to hear the rest."

"I'd rather not," the ECKist said.

"Why not?"

He showed him the piece of paper, and the man caught on right away. "Yeah, I guess I don't want to hear it, either," he said.

## WE'RE NOT IN A RACE

The Golden-tongued Wisdom doesn't come only to ECKists. This happens to people all the time, but not very many are aware of what it means. Nor are many aware of the meaning of their dreams or experiences in their daily life that could be considered waking dreams.

But there is no reason to feel you are falling behind someone else just because you can't understand everything. If you can understand just a little bit, every so often, you are doing well.

On the other hand, if you do gain some insight, through a fortune cookie or anything else, there is no reason to feel you are more spiritual than anyone else. You are on your own path to God. There isn't any hurry. If you think in terms of being slower or faster than someone else, then you are in a race. That is not the path to God.

When you are walking your own path to God, you recognize the message in the kernel of truth that is given to you. The recognition usually comes subtly at first, where you say, "Oh, I see." You may understand the full impact of the message at that point, but more likely than not, it will take longer. Maybe

*The Golden-tongued Wisdom happens to people all the time, but not very many are aware of what it means.*

a couple of weeks later, after you have forgotten about it, something else will happen to bring it back into your consciousness, and it will build on the earlier experience.

## A COMA OF HABITS

Essentially, Soul is asleep in the lower worlds. It is comatose from habits which prevent It from walking the direct path to God. When It is asleep, It does things that cause pain and misery to other people. It may be unfair, unkind, and untrue, because this is the nature of the human consciousness. In ECK we are trying to rise above it, to reach the state of Soul consciousness.

Some ECKists come to a point where they no longer want to be involved with their previous church. Yet others, for one reason or another, need to maintain their ties to the church, often because of their family.

## ECKANKAR'S EXPANSION

In the early days of Eckankar, it was understood that once you took the Second Initiation, you recognized that this commitment to Divine Spirit precluded any other religious affiliation. At this point, it meant you wholeheartedly chose to walk the path of ECK. It was generally accepted that, until you were willing to make this agreement, you would not progress in ECK.

But the teachings are expanding. The consciousness of people today is much broader than it was twenty years ago. It may not be apparent if you judge it by the governing bodies of countries that send their young men off to war. Although there has been an upliftment in consciousness overall, if someone were

*Essentially, Soul is asleep in the lower worlds.*

to ask me when world peace would come about, I would have to say, "Not for a long time."

This universe is not designed for peace, because Soul wouldn't learn anything under those conditions. As long as the lower worlds exist, there will be a place for Satan. You might say he has a duty to accomplish. He is on a mission for God, to create obstacles which will bring about the spiritual upliftment of Soul. If this is the reason Soul is in the lower worlds, then for as long as It is here, Soul will have to face opposition and obstacles that stand between It and Its goals.

## WORLDS OF LIGHT

I am speaking now of the individual as Soul. In the impersonal sense, Soul is neither male nor female. Duality is a lower-world phenomenon that goes as far as the Etheric Plane, which is the high Mental Plane.

Beyond that state, there is no such division, no positive and negative, no shadows. Beyond are the worlds of Light, of pure Love. I am not referring to human love, which has a high side and a low side—warm and giving at its best, possessive and restrictive at its worst. What we are trying to do is gain spiritual freedom from these lower states of the human consciousness.

## OPEN THE DOOR

As I give talks during ECK seminars, there is a certain point at which the door of Soul opens. The first evening is usually a little more difficult. People are winding down from the hardships and hassles of travel and other things. They bring all these tensions into the hall with them and just sit there, tired and jet-lagged.

*In the impersonal sense, Soul is neither male nor female.*

The second night is usually much more relaxed. By Sunday morning, when I give the third talk of the seminar, everything is friendly and very open. I am able to get the message through more directly.

## THREE TYPES OF SPIRITUAL EXERCISES

There are many spiritual exercises in the ECK discourses. Each one opens the person a little bit more to the Sound and Light of God.

I would like to give spiritual exercises for three different groups of people: (1) those who don't dream but want to, (2) those who dream but want to Soul Travel, and (3) those who want to go beyond dreams and Soul Travel to the state of direct knowingness. It's so simple that it may seem as if I'm belittling your intelligence, but I'm not. Truth is always simple.

Just before you go to sleep, sit quietly on your bed. Close your eyes. Chant HU very softly or, if someone is in the room with you, chant it silently to yourself. HU is a special word, the ancient name for God. You could call it the manifested Word or the Sound; it has a power of its own.

*As you take the time to sit there and chant HU, the name of God, you are making a commitment with Divine Spirit.*

As you take the time to sit there and chant HU, the name of God, you are making a commitment with Divine Spirit. Chant HU in a long, drawn-out way for three or four or five minutes, and let yourself settle down. Then wait for a few more minutes before starting the next step.

For those who have been unable to remember their dreams, simply chant the word *dream* spelled out. Chant it out loud, letter by letter: D-R-E-A-M. Do this for about five minutes. Next, chant the same thing quietly for a few minutes, and then just go to sleep. As you are falling asleep, say, "I would like to remember a significant spiritual dream." With this method, you are asking for truth to come through the dream state.

Some of you want Soul Travel, which is usually an advanced state beyond the dream state. Again, sit on your bed or on the floor, shut your eyes, and look into your Spiritual Eye. This is located at a point just above and between the eyebrows. Don't expect to see anything there; just chant HU, the holy name of God.

Then spell out *Soul Travel,* chanting each separate letter: S-O-U-L T-R-A-V-E-L. Do this about three times out loud and then three times quietly.

Those who have Soul traveled may now want to go to the higher state of direct knowingness, without having to go through the intermediary stages. Dreams and Soul Travel are helpful and important, but at some point you outgrow them.

*Divine love brings you all forms of love, including human love.*

Simply chant the words *divine love,* letter by letter. Originally I was going to give it as L-O-V-E, but some people would mix it up with human love. The word *divine* takes it beyond human love. Divine love brings you all forms of love, including human love. To limit it to the usual definition of love is like working from the bottom, instead of working from the top of spirituality.

So, chant D-I-V-I-N-E L-O-V-E. This means you seek the highest form of love, which brings all blessings to you.

*Australian Regional Seminar, Canberra, Australia, Saturday, November 26, 1988*

The Master, in effect, was saying, "All right, you've got a mental knowledge of this quality of God Consciousness. Now let's put it into practice." And so she did.

# 5

# Could I Please Pay for That Honey? Part 2

*A*n ECK initiate's husband, who isn't an ECKist, saw our introductory video "The Journey Home." "I don't think I could handle Eckankar," he told her. "It's too mellow."

## Anything but Mellow

After coming into ECK, the initiate said she had found it anything but mellow. Everything began to change, even her diet and her attitudes about people. She said she used to be able to get away with things. But now, even if she has a bad thought about someone, she feels the effect.

Since there is no way to tell her husband these things, she just stays quiet. "I let him think we're a bunch of mellow people who study a teaching made up of hearts and flowers," she said.

## Rocky Road

Many people do not understand that ECK is a spiritual teaching of substance. One of its features is that it helps the initiates work out a lot of karma.

*Working out karma sometimes takes us down a rocky road.*

Working out karma sometimes takes us down a rocky road. This often happens in ways that no one else knows, because it is our own road.

Occasionally you hear a person say that he would prefer to carry the sorrows of others because they seem lighter than his own. This is sometimes the case in Eckankar, as we get to know our burdens more acutely than ever before. Others usually don't know what we are going through, of course. There is no reason to constantly complain, though we often do until we find it doesn't do much good.

## DISTINCTION OF EXPERIENCE

I sometimes refer to the students of Eckankar as chelas. To those who are new to ECK, *chela* simply means one who is a student of a spiritual teaching. I don't use it too often because the term itself suggests a certain distinction between people—that one is higher or purer than another. This isn't true.

Yet, a person who has studied a spiritual path for many years is going to have more experience in it than a new trainee, even though both are good people, possibly even the same age. So there is a distinction, but it is one of experience.

## GREAT LOVE

A chela in New York was a member of an ECK Satsang class. One evening the Arahata—the Satsang teacher—gave the students an assignment for the next class: "Make a list of all the attributes that you would consider part of God Consciousness." This is the state we are trying to reach—the top of the mountain, the spiritual heights of God.

A few days after the class, the chela listened to an ECK tape where I told a story about an ECKist who was walking on the sidewalk when she was knocked down by a taxicab. The fall broke her arm. A feisty crowd gathered at the scene of the accident and turned against the cabdriver. "Sue him!" they urged her, but the woman refused.

She looked at the distraught cabbie, who was truly concerned as to whether or not she was hurt. She realized he was a husband and a father with a family, and she didn't want to hurt him. She preferred to take her rewards in spiritual value, not in money.

The chela told this story at the next Satsang class. "This, to me, is a person who demonstrates the qualities of God Consciousness," she told the others. "She had love so great that she was able to be more considerate of the cabdriver who ran her down than she was concerned about her own injury."

*"This, to me, is a person who demonstrates the qualities of God Consciousness," she told the others.*

## Put It into Practice

When the class was over, the chela headed for the train station. Suddenly she realized how hungry she was. After she bought a token for the train fare, all she had left was three dollars. It was just enough to buy a sandwich in one of the fast-food shops.

She got herself a chicken sandwich and carried it out to the platform to wait for the train. She stood there thinking about the qualities of God Consciousness, happy that she had been able to contribute to the class discussion. Just then a raggedy-looking young man came up to her. "Please, I'm hungry," he said. "Can you give me some money for food?"

She didn't have any money left, but she did have the sandwich. She wasn't attached to money and wouldn't have minded giving him some if she'd had any. But her food—that was something else. She was really hungry. She would have to think about this.

Finally she said, "Here, take this if you're hungry," and gave him the sandwich. To her this was more of a sacrifice than if she'd had enough money to say, "Take twenty dollars, and buy yourself something good to eat." The food was all she had, so she had to give up what was most dear to her.

The incident taught her something about self-discipline, and it came at the very moment when it could provide the best spiritual opportunity. This is usually how the ECK teachings come to the individual. In this case, it happened when the woman was alone at night on a train platform—cold, tired, and hungry—and someone asked for that which was most precious to her at that moment.

When a scruffy person approaches you on a deserted train platform, the usual reaction is fear. What if this person tries something unruly? But the chela had to neutralize all this in order to recognize the spiritual lesson that was coming. The Master, in effect, was saying, "All right, you've got a mental knowledge of this quality of God Consciousness. Now let's put it into practice." And so she did.

## HEALINGS

Some of the ECK Satsang classes are sponsoring dream workshops for the public. We are gradually beginning to go out into the world to tell others about the teachings of the Light and Sound of God.

An ECKist was going through some personal problems in her life, but at the same time, she enjoyed conducting a series of dream workshops. In one of her classes, she noticed that the people were having all kinds of experiences. Some received healings in unexpected ways.

In one case, a woman complained that her three-

and-a-half-year-old granddaughter had been having horrible nightmares for over three years. "They started when she was about six months old," she told the ECK teacher. "Every single night she wakes up crying about monsters coming after her, and we don't know how to help her. What can we do?"

The ECKist said, "Why not tell your granddaughter that you'll come to her in her dreams and protect her from the monsters?"

The grandmother did just that, and in class the following week she reported the results. "That was the first time my granddaughter didn't wake up crying in the middle of the night. She slept straight through for the first time in over three years."

As you carry the message of ECK to those who are interested and ready for these ancient teachings, healings will occur. You are performing a spiritual service to people who have been looking but haven't found. Some ECKists are even performing a service to their local religious communities.

*As you carry the message of ECK to those who are interested and ready for these ancient teachings, healings will occur.*

## ACTING AS IF

There are ECKists who feel that continuing to participate in their former church will hold them back on the spiritual path. But we must understand that our purpose in Eckankar is to become a Co-worker with God. If we are helping others in their spiritual unfoldment, whether we do it in an ECK-sponsored format or not, then we are acting as if we are Co-workers with God.

"Acting as if" is a principle of ECK. You establish a goal, then act as if the wish is fulfilled and the dream completed. In this way you create your own world.

## GO OUT AMONG PEOPLE

There is an ECKist who plays the piano at a Methodist church. He says he would rather not go to the service, but he finds that through his music people are opened to the Light and Sound of God. He plays anything that fits within the religious atmosphere, mostly happy, uplifting tunes of his own composition.

*He finds that through his music people are opened to the Light and Sound of God.*

He and his wife had just returned from a vacation and were feeling very relaxed. He even looked forward to playing the piano at the Methodist church again. But the first service after his return was a funeral. He wasn't particularly happy about that, but it was part of the job.

The deceased woman had many close friends in the church, and the piano player could feel their sorrow and grief. He warmed up before the service by playing several popular tunes. He found it a discipline to shake off the heavy emotions so that he could keep clear in his playing.

After the service began, he played accompaniment for the soloist and then ended with a light, happy tune. You can't sound too happy during a funeral, but he tried to keep the tone of the music spiritual and enjoyable. He felt good about it because it had been several weeks since he had last played.

The following Sunday, the widower of the deceased woman came over to the piano player. The man said, "Before the service began last week, my stomach was in knots. I was hurting inside so badly that I didn't trust myself to speak. But as you played, the feeling began to be released, and I felt a little bit better. By the end of the service, I even felt as if I might be able to go back out and face the world."

Like the woman who taught the dream class, the

piano player is an example of an ECKist going out among the people to be of service. In the normal course of his life, he found a way to bring the Light and Sound of God to others. They may not be aware that this is happening, but they feel it. Many people come up to him and say, "Your music seems to take me away from here and put me someplace else. It makes me feel happy. And when you stop playing, all of a sudden I'm right back down to earth." This is the main reason the ECKist has continued to play the piano in a Methodist church.

## TRUE SERVICE

The members of a spiritual teaching need to carry something spiritual and uplifting into the world. Without this outflow, they become an introverted group. They become too interested in their own power structure and in pleasing each other within their organization. This is not why Eckankar was formed, and it is not the way the spiritual path of ECK is meant to be.

We have to go out into the world and give of ourselves, but not in a gushy, emotional way. Instead, we give true service to others in the way that they need at the moment. Not as we think they need it, but as Divine Spirit directs us, often using our talents and the things we enjoy doing to accomplish this service.

There are times, though, when a person must be willing to put himself in jeopardy with others in order to give of himself, whether it's to another person or to an animal. And because he is willing to take this on in order to give a service of love, he receives protection.

*The members of a spiritual teaching need to carry something spiritual and uplifting into the world.*

## UNEXPECTED PROTECTION

A veterinarian who worked at a pet hospital got a call from his wife. It was just before closing time. "If you come right home, I can take some packages to the post office," she said.

No more patients were expected, so he tried to shut things down quickly and leave. But just as he was ready to go out the door, one of the birds under his care had an emergency. He stayed to take care of the bird and wasn't able to leave until just after the post office closed. He hoped his wife would understand.

On the way home, he crossed a four-lane highway to get into the left-turn lane. As he approached his turn, he saw that an accident had taken place in the intersection. A car had been hit head-on by a drunk driver. There had been no chance for the car in the left-turn lane to get out of the way. A man and his child had suffered serious injuries.

The ECKist realized that if he hadn't taken the time to tend to the bird, he could have been the one sitting at that intersection when the drunk driver came roaring through.

## MORE THAN MEETS THE EYE

When he made the decision to stay and take care of the bird, he probably worried that his wife would think he cared more about the animals than about her. This is often the type of quandary we are put into. It would be so much easier if things worked out the way they were supposed to, so that we could meet the expectations of others. But when Spirit wants to teach us something about being of service, it is often at our apparent inconvenience.

Yet there is more to it than meets the eye. If we take the extra step to do what we know in our heart

*When Spirit wants to teach us something about being of service, it is often at our apparent inconvenience.*

has to be done, the spiritual understanding and help will come to us.

## SOUL'S EVOLUTION

Birds and other animals need love too. Some human beings have too high an opinion of themselves. They think animals are such a low species that they have no Soul. In ECK we don't refer to Soul as something that we have. Instead we say: I am Soul, and I have a body. Animals are Soul too, and they too have a body.

*Animals are Soul too, and they too have a body.*

Soul moves through the evolutionary process in a number of different forms, including those of animals and birds. These are some of the many different ways in which Soul gains experience, thereby gaining expression of Its divine self. In the process, Soul must learn to receive love and to give love.

To receive love sounds easy enough, but many people have a hard time accepting it from others. This is apparent when someone responds to a gift by saying, "I can't take that." If you were to suggest that their attitude was due to their inability to accept love, they would only deny it. But actions speak louder than words.

## POPCORN AND DUCKS

There is a pond near the ECK Spiritual Center in Minnesota. It's nicely frozen over for ice-skating in winter. In spring there are a number of ducks swimming around in it. One of the ECK staff members liked to walk over to the pond on her breaks. The ducks would come up to her and watch her as she quietly sang HU, a love song to God.

The ducks seemed to enjoy her song. As she walked, they waddled along as fast as they could to

*She didn't understand that they were actually coming to her for love. Not too many gave them spiritual love.*

keep up with her. But one day it occurred to her that they probably expected her to have food for them.

She didn't understand that they were actually coming to her for love. There were plenty of people around to throw food at them, but not too many gave them spiritual love.

She made up her mind to bring them popcorn the next time she came. *They'll really like that,* she thought. At home that evening, she found that her roommate had left half a bag of popcorn in the cupboard. "That's the ECK speaking," she said. "I wanted popcorn for the ducks, and the ECK provided it." She tasted a few pieces, found it a little stale, but decided it was OK for the ducks.

The next day she took the popcorn to work, and at lunchtime she went to the pond to visit the ducks. Some were in the water, and others were walking around on land. She tossed some popcorn at them, but they wouldn't eat it. In fact, they started moving away from her. She followed after them, urging them to eat, convinced they wanted the popcorn.

The ducks that weren't already in the pond headed for the water, and they all swam away, their tails toward her. She was very disappointed, almost to the point of writing those ducks off as foul, ungrateful beasts.

Incidentally, she brought the popcorn that the ducks wouldn't eat back to work and set it on a table. It wasn't too stale for the staff—they ate it all.

A few days later she came back to the pond with toasted whole-grain bread. Seeing two large geese, she figured it must be really hard for them to get food. She tried to give them some of her toast, but they weren't interested. The more she tried, the faster they waddled away from her.

She turned her attention to two ducks standing at the edge of the pond. She threw some toast to them, but they too snubbed her generosity. None of them wanted her food. Disappointed again, she headed back to work.

Suddenly it occurred to her that the ducks had been more congenial when she had showed up just to sing HU to them. She realized then that what they had wanted from her was the love she gave them through chanting HU. Plenty of other people were available to reduce the love to a material substance like bird food, but from her they had come to expect it in its purer form. From this experience, she learned that birds and other animals need love as much as human beings do.

*You become aware by chanting your secret word or HU—not constantly but whenever you think of it.*

The self-discipline involved in a situation like this is to listen, to know and understand the real needs of the beings around us. The discipline is to be aware. You become aware by chanting your secret word or HU—not constantly but whenever you think of it.

## A Gift from a Friend

An ECKist was considered by her friends to be a very emotionally strong individual. She's the kind that others call when they have troubles. No one knows when she has a problem, because she keeps her sorrows to herself. But on the seventeenth anniversary of her father's death, she was feeling very depressed, lonely, forgotten, and unloved.

At work she told her boss how she felt. Fortunately, he was very understanding about it. He said, "On a day like this, sometimes it's better to just forget work and go to some special place or talk with a special person." She had just the person in mind, a very close friend.

She went to her friend's home and found him painting the garage. He had a dog named Buck who was very protective of his owner. The dog didn't like strangers, especially women. When the ECKist sat on the steps to wait for her friend to finish, Buck looked at her and growled. Then he placed himself between her and his master so the man could paint the garage without being bothered. The dog had very definite opinions about women.

The ECKist sat there quietly and watched her friend work. She felt very sad and mellow. She wanted his attention, but she couldn't bring herself to say, "Hey, I feel really down. I need a hug." She needed love, but she didn't know how to ask.

Pretty soon he finished painting the garage. But rather than come over and talk to her, he began to clean his brushes and put things away. The woman just watched him, feeling worse than ever. Buck had gone off somewhere, and she was glad. She didn't need him snarling at her.

Suddenly Buck crept up behind her. She stiffened and waited for him to start his usual growling. Instead, he licked her on the cheek, then sat down beside her and let her pet him.

*A dog is Soul too, and Soul responds to the divine love that comes from the highest plane of God.*

She was amazed at first, until she realized that the dog had understood her need. He came over to give her love, because no one else would give it. In fact, because of her strength, because she couldn't ask, no one else would even expect her to need any love from them.

Buck knew. He was able to give her love. A dog is Soul too, and Soul responds to the divine love that comes from the highest plane of God, through the Holy Spirit, and manifests as Light and Sound.

## ASPECTS OF ECK

There are many different aspects to the ECK teachings. I can't cover the whole field of ECK in each talk, so I try to discuss one area in more depth. Sometimes I'll pick a subject, such as dreams, and pound it until you've had enough for that round. But other times there is a need to talk about the ECK-Vidya (prophecy), healing, learning how to work with the spiritual exercises, protection, and other aspects of ECK.

Right now I would like to mention Soul Travel. Last night I gave a spiritual exercise in three ways: for those who don't dream but wish to dream, for those who dream but wish to Soul Travel, and for those who Soul Travel but wish to go on to direct perception. We always want something a little beyond us. This is the way it should be. The true nature of Soul is to constantly unfold, to keep moving into greater areas of personal awareness.

*The true nature of Soul is to constantly unfold, to keep moving into greater areas of personal awareness.*

## AN UNCOMMON ABILITY

One Second Initiate has the ability to Soul Travel quite often. But once she steps out of her physical body, she rarely makes it out of her apartment. The few times she does get outside, she can't seem to go beyond her own town.

She considers this a problem. It was fine at first, but now she figures there must be more to learn and experience than just walking around her apartment or flying around town.

To Soul Travel is not a common ability. It is one of the things you learn in Eckankar if your interest is along that line. But it's not at all necessary. Some people accomplish the same feat through dream travel. Others totally bypass Soul Travel. They have some dream experiences, then go to the state of direct perception.

This Second Initiate is able to get up in the Soul body, look around, and see her Physical body lying on the bed. In the Soul form she goes into the Astral body, the Astral-Plane counterpart of the Physical body. Everything on earth has its counterpart on the Astral Plane. The buildings and rooms are usually larger and the lighting is slightly different, but essentially things are set up the same way.

When the initiate left her apartment during Soul Travel, she would walk right through the door. You don't have to open a physical door when you're in the Soul body. She would stand in the hallway and begin to call on Wah Z, the Mahanta, the Inner Master. This is the inner side of the Living ECK Master.

Then she would wait for a while. Sometimes he would come around the corner and ask, "Where would you like to go?" She usually said, "I want to go to a Golden Wisdom Temple." But she never got there, because she wasn't ready for it. She still needed the experiences that she was having to bring her the understanding that there must be something more.

## DIMINISH FEAR THROUGH SOUL TRAVEL

*In Soul Travel there is a heightened awareness, another layer of perception beyond the ordinary senses.*

In Soul Travel there is a heightened awareness, another layer of perception beyond the ordinary senses. This added element makes Soul Travel quite an interesting experience.

Some people have only one or two Soul Travel experiences, but it is enough to show them that they are Soul, that they exist beyond the physical body. This is the first step in overcoming the fear of death.

The fear of death usually underlies all the other fears that people have. This is what holds them back in their spiritual life. It is the reason many are failures in their material life. Because of something that happened in the past, maybe in another lifetime, the fear of death lies within the subconscious of the individual.

Once you have the experience of Soul Travel—if this is the route you choose to go—it begins to diminish the fear. Not instantly, of course, because the fear has been built up over a long period of time.

*Once you have the experience of Soul Travel —if this is the route you choose to go— it begins to diminish the fear.*

## USE YOUR OWN CREATIVITY

The initiate wanted greater experiences, and she finally figured out her next step. The Master didn't just come up to her and say, "OK, you don't have to do anything on your own. We'll go off to a Golden Wisdom Temple just because you asked." She realized on her own that, unless she wanted to keep hanging around in her apartment building whenever she got out of the body, she would have to think of a way to change things.

One day she said, "Maybe I should try to do a spiritual exercise while I'm out of the body, to see how it works." This is what she is trying at the present time. It's a good experiment. By not interfering, the Inner Master is forcing her to use her own creativity to expand her awareness.

## A LITTLE SELF-DISCIPLINE

Sometimes we can learn a lot by observing the experiences of other people. When someone else displays a lack of self-discipline, we are usually very quick to pick up on it. "That's why he's a failure in business," we say. "He doesn't keep good records, he doesn't open the store on time, he doesn't answer the phone. It's simply a lack of self-discipline."

*The little self-disciplines that the Inner Master tries to bring into our life are for our own good, our own betterment.*

But all these things that we do in our physical life are actually spiritual lessons. We go through them so that someday we may become a Co-worker with God, one who has learned spiritual self-discipline. The little self-disciplines that the Inner Master tries to bring into our life are for our own good, our own betterment.

## COULD I PLEASE PAY FOR THAT HONEY?

An initiate from Germany sent me an item from a newspaper. It was about an incident that took place when a mother took her bratty little daughter grocery shopping.

They were standing in the checkout line waiting to pay for the groceries. Restless, the little girl put her hands against the cart, which was loaded with food, and shoved it into the back of the woman ahead of them in line.

Once was not enough, of course. She kept on ramming the cart into that poor woman, each time going, "Bam, bam, bam."

Finally the distraught woman turned around and said to the mother, "Could you please ask your daughter to stop it? That hurts."

"I will not," the mother said. "She is being raised in the antiauthoritarian way. I wish her to have freedom." In the meantime, the little girl kept right on banging the cart into the woman's back — bam, bam, bam.

About that time, the man behind the mother and daughter started to open a jar of honey. The other customers saw him doing it, but no one really thought anything of it. He gave the lid a final twist, removed it from the jar, and stepped up to the little girl. Then very slowly he began to pour the honey all over the top of her head.

The jar of honey was half-empty before the shocked mother could speak. "What are you doing?" she sputtered. "Stop! Stop doing that to my little girl!"

"I will not," the man said firmly. "I was raised in the antiauthoritarian way."

Everybody laughed except the mother. She was just outraged. As the last couple of drops fell onto the little girl's head, someone at the back of the line called out, "Could I please pay for that honey?"

## GOD CONSCIOUSNESS

For over a year I have been working on a book, the third in a series. The first one was *The Wind of Change*, then came *Soul Travelers of the Far Country*. This one is called *Child in the Wilderness*.

The book actually is an account of God Consciousness. It also addresses the misconceptions people have about God Consciousness, what they expect of those who have it, and how their expectations are often wrong. The book was structured to be a graphic example of how God Consciousness works.

*The book was structured to be a graphic example of how God Consciousness works.*

We usually expect a story to start at a certain level, gain speed, finally reach a peak, then come to a conclusion. Everything comes neatly together, and the story is over.

Most people would expect the same thing from a story about the experience of reaching God Consciousness: After a series of events, the person is deposited on top of the mountain of God, and that's the end of the story.

## WHAT HAPPENS NEXT?

But what happens then? Does he remain there forever?

The difficult part was trying to structure the book so that the reader would understand what can happen to an individual's life when the experience occurs. He walks along in his daily life, then all of a sudden events begin to escalate. They carry him higher spiritually, turn him upside down, and turn the social structure inside out.

Then, once the individual has reached the top of the mountain, equally important is his descent down the other side, back into everyday living. There has to be a change. It doesn't happen the same way with everyone, of course.

Perhaps 10 percent of what actually occurred is in the book, but then writing is a form of shorthand. You can't express everything, so you have to select very carefully to bring out the salient points.

Most of you have a long way to go home, so I won't belabor our farewell. Have a safe journey home. I am always with you.

*Once the individual has reached the top of the mountain, equally important is his descent down the other side, back into everyday living.*

*1988 Australian Regional Seminar,*
*Canberra, Australia,*
*Sunday, November 27, 1988*

The golden cup is Soul. The more the ECK flows in and out of the cup, the more Soul shines with Its own Golden Light.

# 6

# DREAMLAND: HAVE IT YOUR WAY, PART 1

The dream worlds—and there are many—are as real as this physical world. You can make full use of the hours your body is asleep. You can go to the other worlds, look around, and learn. It does not have to be a time of zero consciousness; it can be a very fruitful and interesting experience.

## YOUR DREAM WORLDS ARE REAL

It is during this period of sleep that you, as Soul, move into the heavenly worlds of God and explore. The Mahanta, which is the inner side of myself, or one of the other ECK Masters generally comes along with you. We act as guides to make sure that you don't get lost in one of the many locales.

In some of the inner worlds, just as here, there are people who would try to pull you off the spiritual path. But there is always a spiritual guide nearby to insure your safety.

## SEEING TRUTH DIFFERENTLY

Often when people come to ECK and confront the dreamland, they realize that there is something to

*It is during this period of sleep that you, as Soul, move into the heavenly worlds of God and explore.*

the inner worlds, to the spiritual planes of ECK. But their conditioning is such that they are ashamed of their association with Eckankar and the Mahanta, the Living ECK Master. Their training from childhood has dictated that truth must be viewed in a certain way. Anything that doesn't line up with that idea of truth is to be ridiculed or put completely out of their thoughts.

*The social consciousness is very strong as a person grows up.*

The social consciousness is very strong as a person grows up. If your family and friends share beliefs that are different from your own, they might hold you up to ridicule. They might do it because of your acceptance of the ECK teachings, the ECK environment, the ECK society.

Because of this, as you come into ECK you question your choice: Am I really walking a true path, or is this another diversion into the wild blue yonder? Am I making a fool of myself?

Your family and friends will work on your doubts, of course. "Do you really know what you're doing? Are you sure this is what you want?" And the doubts begin to grow stronger.

At about this point, you get the pink slip for your Second Initiation in ECK. Now you have to make a decision: Am I ready for ECK? Or should I stay in my old religion?

## PRACTICE LOVE

This is often a very difficult time. You feel you are separating yourself from the life you lived before, although this isn't necessary. Of course, as your beliefs change there is bound to be some degree of separation. Two people become friends because they have things in common. All of a sudden you have new attitudes and beliefs; you want to run your life in a new way. The people you used to associate with no longer seem to fit into your world in the same way as before.

But rather than taking the path of alienation or estranging yourself from your family and friends, you can use this as an opportunity to practice divine love. You can live your life and still allow them the freedom to believe what they will.

This is not always easy for new converts to any religious teaching. They often become very aggressive in presenting the teachings and tell others more than they ever cared to know. This can cause hard feelings. It can set up an enmity between the convert and the group of people he left.

This feeling is not necessary if an individual is able to practice patience and forbearance. An ECKist needs to understand that his former associates are very afraid of what's going to happen to them in their afterlife. Their religion does not teach them to have the same kind of experience that an ECK initiate has.

By the time you complete two years of study and are ready for the Second Initiation, you generally will have had at least one experience with the Light or the Sound of God. It will come in the dream state, or even through an outer experience. It will let you know that the path of ECK is real.

*Their religion does not teach them to have the same kind of experience that an ECK initiate has.*

## LEAVING THE BEATEN PATH

Many of us live in a Christian society. So we find that Christians often try to get you back into the fold. One of the methods is to express concern that you'll go to hell if you don't return to the church.

More than concern about you, I think they have grave misgivings about their own destination. They aren't sure what's going to happen to them when they die. They project this fear on anyone who dares to leave the beaten path.

Stepping off into what they consider the unknown is a fearful thing, and the fear is based on a lack of experience in the other worlds. The best way to begin to get this experience is through the dream state.

## GETTING THE NEWS

A listener called in to a radio-talk-show host in Minneapolis. The caller wanted to make it known that the Judgment was coming the next day. The talk-show host replied, "If the Judgment is scheduled for tomorrow, we'll get it right here. Get the news while it's news!"

Listening to them, I had a vision of how it would be on that particular judgment day. All the newsmen would run out to get man-on-the-street interviews — "What is your reaction to this last day on earth?" — and plan to run the videotape on the six o'clock news.

Lately Eckankar has been in the forefront of the media in Minneapolis. Newspeople have been coming to the Eckankar Spiritual Center to take pictures and find out who we are. They express curiosity about basic aspects of ECK such as Soul Travel. It frightens some of them. "What is it?" they ask.

## WE LEARN BY EXPERIENCE

One way to explain it is that, just as a dream is a true inner experience, Soul Travel is a more vivid inner experience. These are all spiritual experiences, and each brings us a greater awareness of our spiritual self and our spiritual capabilities — what we can or cannot do. In ECK we learn by experience; we do something.

*Stepping off into what they consider the unknown is a fearful thing, and the fear is based on a lack of experience in the other worlds.*

The Law of Karma works in a certain way for most people who are not in ECK. A curtain stands between cause and effect. In ECK, very soon after you do something that hinders you or someone else spiritually, the curtain is pulled up and the deed comes right back at you. It happens quickly enough to be within reach of your memory so that you can learn from it. Sometimes the act comes back so fast that the only way to miss the lesson would be to develop total amnesia.

In other teachings, where the Light and Sound of God is not as direct, the curtain between cause and effect stays down much longer. For instance, a person becomes very angry at work, blows off at someone else, and gets away with it. So he does the same thing to a second person, a third person, and soon he gains a reputation as a man who is not to be crossed. He rises to the top of the corporate ladder, a belligerent person admired by all.

In our society, people are admired for reaching the heights of material success, no matter how they got there. Only when such a person begins to fall do others come out of the woodwork. It's just as the Hindu proverb says: "When an elephant is in trouble, even a frog will kick him." But because the curtain stayed down for so long, he probably doesn't remember what he did to turn everyone against him.

## THE BALLOON RACE

An ECKist who completed two years of study received the pink slip for her Second Initiation, and that night she had a dream. People outside of ECK usually don't understand that our inner and outer lives are very closely connected. If something significant happens out here, then something is going on

> *In ECK, very soon after you do something that hinders you or someone else spiritually, the curtain is pulled up and the deed comes right back at you.*

*There is always a connection between the inner and outer events.*

inwardly. In the case of an ECK initiation, the inner experience may come before the individual receives the pink slip on the outer, it may come on the same day, or it may come later. There is always a connection between the inner and outer events.

In the dream the ECKist was up on a hill, deep in conversation with a man who was considered an outcast of society. The members of the community were crowded below. As they looked up and watched the woman and the outcast talk, they grew angry, more judgmental. How dare this person, this ECKist, keep company with someone they had cast out of their society!

After they finished their conversation on the hill, the dreamer knew she had better flee. She ran partway down the hill to a cave. She hid there for a while, but she knew they would find her if she stayed much longer. Seeing a pile of garments, she quickly covered herself and prepared to escape.

Just then the crowd entered the cave and pulled her out. An angry confrontation followed. After much debate, the leader of the group told her, "Our religion is greater than yours, and we're going to prove it.

"We'll have a balloon race," he said. "You'll have a balloon, we'll have a balloon, and we'll just see whose goes higher." As chief of the community, he decided he would be the one to race against her.

The leader of the group and the dreamer climbed into their balloons, and soon they were up in the air. All of a sudden the ECKist's balloon changed in appearance. It became larger and rose higher. The other balloon reached a certain height and just kind of skimmed along the treetops, while the ECKist soared high and free.

Then the race was over, and both balloons were back on the ground. The people crowded around to claim victory. The ECKist tried to explain that she had gone higher.

"No!" they insisted. "The person from our community flew higher and faster." The ECKist knew that just the opposite was true, but the people hadn't been able to see the situation clearly from the ground.

When she woke up, she wondered what the dream meant. What was it trying to tell her?

Finally she realized that the individual she had talked with on the hill was the Mahanta, who generally is an outcast of traditional religious society. She had felt very keenly the disapproval of the people around her.

The balloons represented the spiritual beliefs of the ECKist and those of the orthodox religious community. When her balloon flew higher, according to the rules of the contest, the ECKist won. From her viewpoint, her path was more appropriate and took her higher. The others, of course, didn't see it that way.

This is how it often is in ECK. Even though you know that the teachings of ECK are real, that the experiences with the Light and Sound of God are valid, other people don't think in terms of actual experience.

*Experience is more important than belief, because only through experience can we learn what is true and what is not true.*

Experience is more important than belief, because only through experience can we learn what is true and what is not true. But experience is merely a halfway step to awareness. We are not just seeking experience for its own sake. The purpose of dream and Soul Travel experiences is to reach a greater awareness of life and our place in it, of who and what we are as Soul.

## COOL DOWN

An ECKist in Australia had another kind of experience. We call it a waking dream. She teaches French to students about seven or eight years of age.

It was a hot, sultry day. With each passing hour the children grew more unruly. She tried every trick she could think of to maintain order in the classroom, but nothing worked. She thought the day would never end.

To make matters worse, a train strike was in progress at this time. Instead of the usual ten-minute train ride home, she had to wait for a bus and endure a several-hour ride. All the buses were overcrowded because of the strike, and none of them had air conditioning. The teacher was not having a good day.

As she sat on the bus seething about the events of the day, a communication came through on the driver's radio. Straining her ears to listen in, she heard a voice say, "The needle on my temperature gauge is going up. What should I do?" She realized it was another bus driver talking to command center.

"Is the needle in the yellow zone or the red?" a voice at command center asked.

"It's in the red," the driver said.

"Well, slow down," command center instructed him. "Let the engine cool down."

The transmission had a dual purpose. It was the ECK, the Holy Spirit, trying to tell the teacher, "Hey, cool down. Take it easy. The students were unruly because it was a hot day, and you're going to need more patience to get through it." She didn't get the message, though.

A little while later her own bus driver swung the crowded vehicle around the corner. He was moving right along, trying to make good time. But three

*It was the ECK, the Holy Spirit, trying to tell the teacher, "Hey, cool down. Take it easy."*

teenagers were standing in the street, and they wouldn't get out of the way.

"Some people won't move even if you drive over their toes," the bus driver griped. He saw that he had no choice but to slow down. When he came to a stop, the teenagers finally moved out of the way, and the bus was able to proceed.

Again, the ECK was trying to tell her, "Give up your anger. Slow down, and just let it go." But she couldn't hear it.

The bus driver put on his right-turn signal. Just as he was about to start the turn, a car pulled up on his right side and tried to squeeze past. The bus came to an abrupt stop, and the driver leaned out the window. "You gotta be joking!" he yelled at the car. "Can't you see the signal?"

The words finally triggered something in the ECKist. "You must be joking," she repeated to herself. "Can't you see the signal?" Suddenly she understood the simple message that the Master was sending her: Leave your anger in the classroom. Don't take it home with you. Cool off.

*Spiritual awareness will let you know when and how to listen.*

This is a very simple example of a waking dream. Things like this go on all the time in your everyday life. They pop up regularly to help you through your life, and spiritual awareness will let you know when and how to listen.

## LIFE'S COGWHEELS

Most people don't recognize these incidents when they occur. If they do get a glimmer that something has taken place, they often just laugh about it. They consider it one of those quirks that happens now and then.

But all of life is interconnected. Like a series of

cogwheels in an old-fashioned clock, everything moves together. Most people are aware only of their own circumference; they ignore everything outside their own little area of the world.

As you go further in ECK, you develop a greater awareness of what and who you are. You learn where your circle begins and ends, and where the circles of other people begin and end. You then begin to realize that when you act in a certain manner, you are being cause. You are setting up effects that touch the circles of other people.

Whether you meant to do it or not is irrelevant; what counts is that you did it. The doer of a thoughtless action will reap the consequences of that action. As an ECKist, you often reap the consequences very quickly.

*The doer of a thoughtless action will reap the consequences of that action.*

## ABORTION QUESTION

A young ECKist told me about a friend of hers who got pregnant. The friend didn't really want to have the child out of wedlock while she was still in high school, so she considered having an abortion.

After giving it a lot of thought, she decided to have the abortion. She got the name and number of a clinic that was supposed to counsel her and asked the ECKist to come with her. But when they arrived for the girl's appointment, they found a clinic run by a Christian group that was zealously antiabortion.

Some of the staff members came to take the young lady to another room. The ECKist saw right through them; she knew that the clinic's advertisement had misrepresented their motives. "They're going to try to scare the wits out of you," she cautioned her friend. "They're going to try to frighten you into changing your mind."

When the teenager came back out to the lobby, she told the ECKist, "I'm glad you warned me. If you hadn't, I wouldn't have been prepared for their scary film and their strong pitch. I don't know if I could have handled it."

But she made the choice to have an abortion, and eventually it was done.

There are strong social forces surrounding this issue. On the one hand you have the pro-life/anti-abortion advocates, and on the other, the forces of pro-choice — a woman's right to make her own choice. I got to thinking it over, to fine-tune my own views, and this is my position.

Suppose the fetus is allowed to come so close to term that it would be able to breathe the first breath of life on its own after it is delivered. If a doctor were to end its existence at that late stage, I would have to call it the taking of life.

*Soul enters the body at the time of the first breath. The fetus is not Soul.*

But in the first several months of pregnancy, a fetus is not developed to the point where it could breathe. Its heart and lungs are underdeveloped; the breath of life has not come in.

A person knows very early on that she is pregnant, and my feeling is this: If one is going to have an abortion, the time to exercise that freedom of choice is before the first breath of life comes in. Soul enters the body at the time of the first breath. The fetus is not Soul.

## DUST TO DUST

We are living in changing times. Decisions like this come up often, and people are confused about what is right and what is wrong. But even the Bible says that the Lord God breathed into man the breath of life, and man became a living Soul.

When the physical body dies, Soul goes immediately into the other worlds in full consciousness.

To take the point further, when the physical body dies, Soul goes immediately into the other worlds in full consciousness. It continues Its existence without interruption. The physical body does not resurrect. The body returns to the dust of the earth and stays there.

This is a great area of ignorance in many orthodox religions. A school of thought in Christianity is that the body rests in the ground until the Judgment Day. At that time, even though it has been munched on by who knows what, the physical body will miraculously rise again.

To me, this is not a spiritual belief. It is not based on reality. It is not true. A lot of people will object to that, but Christians can find the answer in their own scriptures, if they will read it with right understanding.

## DOORWAYS FOR SOUL

Until Soul comes into the body with the first breath of life, the body is just a physical machine. With that first breath of life the body becomes the temple of Soul, to be treated with all respect. At this point we have a great reverence for life; but until this point, it isn't life as occupied by Soul.

There are many jokes about how pregnant women develop strange cravings for different foods. Keep in mind that the Soul waiting to be born was in a physical body before, probably not too long ago, and may have enjoyed things like pickles and ice cream.

The pregnant woman starts to build an affinity with the Soul waiting to use her body as a doorway into the physical plane. Much of this takes place in the dream state. The mother's inner agreement to accommodate the Soul's dietary tastes manifests in these strange cravings. It's like she's saying, "Anything for my baby. Got a taste for pizza? I'll go get some right now."

So, contrary to what many people would like to believe, these cravings do not indicate a nutritional need. The mother could get along very well with the nutritional program set up by her doctor. The cravings are influenced by the Soul who is going to reincarnate as her child.

## MASTER PAINTER

Everything that occurs in life—even the strange cravings of a mother-to-be—has a greater meaning. It's as if a master painter were painting life, putting a little touch here and a little touch there.

We can't always understand what that little dab of green or brown is all about. But as the master painter puts more and more of the picture together, we begin to see that each little brushstroke means something. Each has a relation to something else.

Some people envision the inner planes as being stacked up like pancakes. As illustrated in the ECK God Worlds chart, which is for informational purposes only, the green pancake on the bottom is the Physical Plane, the pink above it is the Astral Plane, the orange on top of that is the Causal Plane, and the blue is the Mental Plane.

An individual doesn't usually take off like a rocket from the green pancake to the orange one. In the dream state the movement from one plane to the other is often so gentle that you don't know it has happened. It's like the times you wake up and remember doing something or talking to someone but can't recall if it occurred in a dream or out here. It may take a while to realize that it happened in the dream.

*Everything that occurs in life— even the strange cravings of a mother-to-be—has a greater meaning.*

We have errands to do on the other planes, but most people aren't aware of it. I see you there, sometimes meet with you, or sometimes just wave hello and keep going. Each of us is busy doing something for the divine purpose of God, the Sugmad.

## THROUGH THE ENERGY FIELD

One time I was visiting the Mental Plane. I had made an appointment to meet with an ECK chela on a certain street on the Astral Plane. So at the appointed time, I left the Mental Plane and came straight through to that particular place in the pink pancake.

The initiate was waiting when I arrived. We greeted each other and started walking down the street. Suddenly we passed through an invisible curtain to a higher plane. Nothing seemed to change, but there was a slightly different sensation, like going through an energy field. The chela didn't notice it.

As we continued our walk, the familiar twentieth-century scenery changed. We found ourselves in a setting right out of the old American West. Up ahead we saw Conestoga wagons — the covered wagons used by the settlers when they moved out West to establish new homesteads.

Soul always works in the present moment, and the past and future are all contained in the present. We think of the past as something that is gone, a dead image. This is so in a way, but at the same time, the past is still occurring in the Causal memory. When you get there, it looks as real as anything you normally consider to be in your present.

The potential for the future is the other side of the present moment. As Soul stands on a promontory in the present moment, It can look at the past or future.

The chela and I had gone through an energy field, and at this point we were on the Causal Plane. "We have to establish the time frame of this experience," I said, observing the covered wagons and pioneers prodding their oxen down a rutted road. *Probably the Oregon Trail,* I thought.

Experiences on the inner planes rarely come with signposts that announce the exact date. Nor can you count on someone running up to you and saying, "Hi, how are you? It's 1865." If you are interested in finding out how to fit into the framework of the experience, you have to use your wits and creativity to figure out what's going on.

Off to the right a grizzled old man stood in front of a ramshackle storefront. He had on a slouch hat and raggedy clothing, with a worn pipe hanging from his mouth. *He looks like one of those settlers who came west from Kentucky,* I thought.

I waved at him as we passed by. "Seen a lot of those wagons going by lately?" I called out. It was a subtle way of trying to find out the year.

"Yep," he said. "Folks didn't use 'em as much before the war."

War? He must mean the Civil War, I figured. That was a point of reference for many years after it was over.

"But you see a lot of 'em these last fifteen years," he continued.

*The Civil War ended in 1865,* I thought, and according to the old settler, fifteen years had passed. "This must be about 1880," I said to the initiate.

I pointed out that we had to be careful about the way we asked questions of these people. "Our clothes

*Experiences on the inner planes rarely come with signposts that announce the exact date.*

look the same to us as they did before, but to them we appear to be dressed like everybody else. They would not feel too comfortable around you if you were to ask outright, 'What year is this?' "

We said good-bye to the old man and continued down the road. After a while we came to some caverns. I led the chela inside and showed him an underground city — an entirely different setting than the one we had just left.

*The other planes have various regions and cultures, too, just as we have here on earth.*

The other planes have various regions and cultures, too, just as we have here on earth. Sometimes they are so different from each other that the traveler can't tell where he is. It would be similar to an alien landing in an Eskimo village, then going to New York City. He would probably wonder if he was on the same planet.

I guided the initiate along an underground walkway that took us back to theAstral Plane. From there he was able to wake up back in his physical body, but he wasn't aware that anything had taken place.

I'm always a little disappointed when a person who has an experience like this writes and says, "I can't remember my dreams. Is there something you can do to help?" I'm tempted to write back and just say, "1880."

## An Exercise for Dream Recall

An ECK chela told me about a spiritual exercise he uses to remember dreams. As he goes to bed at night, he visualizes a golden goblet on his nightstand. Then he says, "When I go to sleep and have a dream experience, the ECK is going to fill this cup with the Light and Sound of God."

In this way, each dream or inner experience the

chela has fills the cup a little bit, then a little bit more.

Upon awakening in the morning, the dreamer does another short spiritual exercise. He visualizes himself drinking liquid from the cup on his nightstand. The liquid is made of the Light and Sound, and he drinks it all.

After he used this visualization technique for a while, he began to notice that the cup became increasingly brighter every day. It seemed to have more life.

In contemplation he asked what this meant. The Mahanta answered: "The golden cup is Soul. The more the ECK flows in and out of the cup, the more Soul shines of Its own Golden Light."

I think you will find this a very helpful spiritual exercise. May the blessings be.

*ECK Springtime Seminar, San Diego, California, Friday, March 24, 1989*

You can go back, pick up the key—the tool, talent, or lesson from a previous lifetime—and bring it into the present. You can then use it to help you walk the spiritual path to God today.

# 7

# DREAMLAND: HAVE IT YOUR WAY, PART 2

*I* talk to people who care about reality and truth, and what this all means. Some of my talk themes are: How does this life relate to the invisible world? How can we reach the invisible world? And once there, how can we bring back anything useful for this life?

We don't want to become dwellers on the inner threshold who can't handle life out here. How can we learn through dream study to become more useful citizens in the outer world? This is what we are to do.

## AN EVER-BRIGHTER VEHICLE

Last night I gave a spiritual exercise which I will repeat briefly. Every evening at bedtime, visualize a golden cup near you which is to be filled with your dream experiences. When you awake in the morning, in contemplation or in your imagination, drink from the cup. You are drinking in the experiences. It is a conscious way of saying, I want to remember what I'm doing on the inner planes while my body is asleep.

The golden cup is Soul; it is you. As you put more attention on drinking from the cup, it takes on a life of its own. It grows brighter. The more the ECK flows

*Every evening at bedtime, visualize a golden cup near you which is to be filled with your dream experiences.*

in and out of the cup, the more Soul shines of Its own golden light. You, as Soul, become an ever-brighter vehicle for the Holy Spirit.

This is how to have it your own way, because Soul is unique. There is no other like you. And the experiences you have lead to a singular awareness of the relationship between your life and its divine meaning.

## DREAMLAND IS REAL

*Physical and spiritual awareness are cut of the same divine cloth. The physical is burlap; the spiritual is silk.*

Most people consider dreams as merely imagination. Yet the physical and spiritual awareness are cut of the same divine cloth. The physical is burlap; the spiritual is silk.

While the body sleeps, we leave it for the inner worlds. The time spent there is called a dream. A dream is a memory of our activities on the inner planes. It can be recalled clearly or with distortions. At first, most people see their inner life in symbols or in fragments.

We can also view the ECK-Vidya in our dreams. This is the ancient science of prophecy. The ECK-Vidya works because the inner and outer worlds are interconnected. Experiences that happen on the physical plane may occur on the inner, and experiences on the inner planes may also occur on the outer.

## A TALL ORDER

The Living ECK Master wants to teach people: (1) just to dream; (2) once they dream, to separate their mental distortions from an authentic inner experience; and (3) how to travel in and out of the body in full consciousness.

This is a tall order. First, he must overcome people's fear.

Many of you write to me about your experiences.

Some of you are very honest about what you learned from them. If there is a useful point in it, I may pass a certain experience along to others, without identifying you.

## WHEN THINGS GO WRONG

Too often a person tries to order the ECK around. It usually happens when something goes wrong. The situation works on your nerves until you've had it up to here. That's when you start to throw some anger at the Mahanta or the ECK.

But after a while you find out that this may not be a good idea. You need only compare your results with those of someone who got through the same situation without the anger. Here's an example.

One cold morning a man left his house to go to work, but his car wouldn't start. Although the engine cranked over, it didn't quite catch. "Anytime now," he said, trying again and again. He didn't want to flood the engine or run the battery down, but the car kept teasing him, coughing just enough to make him think it would catch on the next try.

Pretty soon he got angry. Speaking very personally to the Mahanta, he said, "Where are you when I need you? What is this ECK stuff? Just when a person needs It, It doesn't work." He also threw in a few choice words, forgetting that ECK is the path of the Blue Light, not blue words.

## OR YOU CAN LAUGH

In another part of town, his wife was having the same problem. But unlike her husband's car—stuck in a nice, safe place—hers had stalled in the middle of a busy street some distance away from home.

She got out of the car to evaluate the situation

*Too often a person tries to order the ECK around. It usually happens when something goes wrong.*

and suddenly started laughing. It struck her as quite funny to be stopped in the middle of the street, traffic driving around her.

Soon another driver came by and offered to push her car out of the traffic. When she was safely on the side of the road, he gave her the name of the garage he used. "They'll take care of you," he said. "They'll do a good job."

This wasn't the first time she'd had problems with her car. Recently her husband had suggested she take it to a certain service station. Two mechanics had looked it over thoroughly. Finally they told her, "We don't know what's wrong with it." She had paid them for their time, and now the car was stuck in the street far from home.

This time she went to the garage recommended by the helpful driver. The mechanics found the problem and told her, "We can fix it for you right away. In the meantime, we'll give you a ride home."

Meanwhile, back at the ranch, the husband was running out of words. He finally called a tow truck to jump start the car, pacing back and forth impatiently as he waited. The inner voice of the Master said, "Stay by the phone" — but he had this urge to go out to his car and recite a few leftover words.

The phone rang while he was outside; he didn't hear it. It was the towing company calling back to make sure he still needed them. When he didn't answer, they figured he had left home and everything was OK.

The husband waited for a while then went back inside to call the towing company again. "We'll get somebody out there as soon as we can," they promised. They came an hour later and got his car going. He arrived at work very, very late.

*The inner voice of the Master said, "Stay by the phone."*

## WHAT AN INCONVENIENCE MEANS SPIRITUALLY

Luckily the man was able to recognize the lesson. "I have a lot further to go in my spiritual unfoldment than I thought," he said. He didn't know that, just by realizing this, he was a lot further along than he thought.

This is an example of the waking dream. When outer events reflect a spiritual lesson, it often comes in the form of an inconvenience. So whenever an incident occurs that causes you inconvenience, try to stop for a minute. Look it over and ask, "What's behind this experience?" There is a spiritual lesson every time.

*Whenever an incident occurs that causes you inconvenience, try to stop for a minute. Look it over and ask, "What's behind this experience?"*

## A LABOR OF SISYPHUS

Some of you may be familiar with the phrase "a labor of Sisyphus," which generally refers to an unending task. It is based on a story in Greek mythology. The greedy king of Corinth was condemned in the afterlife to repeatedly roll a great stone up a steep hill. Every time he got it to the summit, the stone would slip away and roll to the bottom of the hill. Over and over he would have to trudge back down, find the fallen rock, and once again start pushing it up the hill.

As you unfold spiritually, you often experience little incidents—the car that won't start, the light that burns out—that feel like labors of Sisyphus. No matter how hard you try to get something accomplished, the stone slips away and you have to start all over again. "Master, how long can this go on?" you ask. Actually, quite a long time.

There is a spiritual lesson incorporated in the story of the king of Corinth. Soul keeps pushing the stone up the hill, trying to reach the spiritual heights. As soon as It gets there, It finds the stone is too heavy, the load is too great. Soul loses Its grip and then has to start all over again.

This is called reincarnation. And it's a slow process that we would like to do without, as soon as possible.

## By Hard Experience

I had lunch with a few friends recently. "What's happening to the video arcades?" I asked them. "I've noticed in the last few years that not as many people go to these places."

"More people are buying home computer games," one of our group said. "They are very instructive and a lot of fun. Some really good games are available now. One is called Zelda II: The Legend of Link."

The hero in this home computer game is called Link. Link goes from level to level, through many worlds, meeting all kinds of opposition. One of his obstacles is a bush. By using the right tool, he finds the secret passageway that takes him to another level.

Even if you can't use the tool on a certain level, you keep it for possible future use. Eventually you realize that you can't get past level three without a tool picked up on level one. You learn by hard experience, by playing the game again and again.

## Soul's Total Experience

It is very much the same as the spiritual experience in reincarnation. In each incarnation we pick up tools —we learn a particular lesson or develop a certain skill. But the problem is this: As we go into succeeding lifetimes, we forget what we have learned before.

*In each incarnation we pick up tools— we learn a particular lesson or develop a certain skill.*

If we only knew how to tap into our total experience as Soul, we could look to the past and draw upon a tool once mastered but now forgotten. We could bring that tool into this lifetime and use it to solve a problem that is holding us back on the spiritual path, a problem that is preventing us from going to the next level.

## PRESENT TOOLS

People outside of ECK generally get the tools by continuing to reincarnate—a very slow process. In ECK we want to take a more direct route. This is why I teach dream and Soul Travel techniques.

*In ECK we want to take a more direct route. This is why I teach dream and Soul Travel techniques.*

If you run into a block that keeps you from getting to the next level of initiation, you can go back; pick up the tool, talent, or lesson from a previous lifetime; and bring it into the present. You can then use it to help you walk the spiritual path to God today.

The creators of these computer games often have a deep insight into how life works. The games are constructed almost like a self-taught course in spiritual principles. Of course, the games give you only a secondhand, electronic experience. The best way to learn is to go out into the world, at least part of the time, getting your own experiences.

## DREAM MESSAGE

Sometimes a lesson derived from the dream state brings a healing. An ECK initiate went to see her doctor about a certain health problem. He gave her two prescriptions which had proven helpful to other patients with the same condition. She took the medications faithfully for a few days but finally concluded that they were not going to work for her.

One night she had a dream—a very simple inner

experience. First she saw a plain black screen. Then letters began to appear, one by one, each a different color, spelling out the word *Ornade*. She didn't know exactly what it was, but she had a feeling it was significant for her health. She woke up in the middle of the night and, while the experience was fresh in her mind, she got out of bed and carefully wrote down the word.

The next day she called the pharmacist who filled her prescriptions. "Is there a drug called Ornade?" she asked.

"Yes, there is," he said. "It's often used as a decongestant." As far as he knew, it had never been used as a remedy for her particular condition.

A few days later she went to see her doctor again. "The drugs you prescribed don't work for me," she said. "I would like to try Ornade."

"It won't help you at all," he said. "It's perfectly useless for your condition."

She felt foolish, but she told him about seeing the name in a dream. She was very persistent about wanting to give it a try, and finally he gave in. "All right," he said. "I don't recommend it, but it won't hurt you."

He wrote her out a prescription. She went directly to the pharmacy to have it filled and began to use the drug that same day. In a short time she found that it worked very well for her, even though it was not intended as a treatment for her condition.

## CROSSING THROUGH A CURTAIN

Sometimes the inner message from the Mahanta comes through quite clearly, just like a sign. Other times it comes through in symbols or fragments. It pretty much depends on the dreamer's perception.

*Sometimes the inner message from the Mahanta comes through quite clearly, just like a sign.*

The Spiritual Exercises of ECK help clear out distortions from your dreams. The inner experiences are every bit as real as the ones you are having here. But the inner experience has to cross through a curtain. It's like pushing it through cheesecloth. By the time it gets through to the waking state, some of the basic elements are lost or scrambled. If you don't write it down right away, it goes away very quickly.

*The Spiritual Exercises of ECK help clear out distortions from your dreams.*

The same woman also had another dream. Over breakfast the following morning she told her husband about it. "You received a check in the mail for either twenty-two or twenty-four hundred dollars," she said. "And you gave me six hundred dollars out of it." She was very proud of remembering the dream so clearly.

He looked at her in surprise and started laughing. Then he left the kitchen and came back with a check for $2,440.00. Because her dream had been so accurate, he said, "Six hundred is for you."

Not all your dreams will work out as well and turn a profit. But sometimes they turn out surprisingly well for you, and that makes it fun.

## DREAM HUNTER

I encourage experiences in the dream state because it is such an interesting place. As you live, move, and have your being on the inner planes during the night while your body sleeps, you meet different people and see many different places. Sometimes the experiences are fantastic and enjoyable, but above all, they are highly educational.

Usually the experiences are spiritual, though at times they come through as nightmares. What you have to do then is pursue the nightmare. Don't be the pursued; become the pursuer, become the hunter. Find out why this is happening to you, why you are having this nightmare.

It might come through as a dream where you are being chased by animals or certain people. Generally this means you are being made to face a fear of some kind which developed in a past life.

*Find out why this is happening to you, why you are having this nightmare.*

## TWISTS OF HUMAN NATURE

People tend to get up in arms when you discuss an emotionally charged topic, especially if their position on it is different than yours. Often their position has nothing to do with reason; it's based on pure emotion. But emotion can be much more powerful than reason, because emotion is often blind. Some people can't see or talk straight if you present a position different from theirs.

The concept of original sin is one of the foundations of Christianity. People who follow this belief take it for granted that they are spiritually corrupt at birth. They have been taught to believe this from the cradle, and they accept it in themselves. Because of this, they have negative thoughts about themselves.

Although they can accept this general imperfection in themselves, don't ever call them intolerant or imply that they are prone to anger. If you do, they're bound to become angry and intolerant. This is one of the peculiar little twists about human nature. Usually I try to be careful not to tease people who express such attitudes.

## FIGHTING FOR GOD

At times I see certain truths not generally accepted by the orthodox mind. When people become emotionally charged over an issue, it's often because they don't know their own scriptures. And if they don't know them, they cannot practice them. So often the doctrine of love set forth in the Christian Bible falls by the wayside, totally disregarded.

Some people become defenders of Christianity, apparently feeling that there is no divine power behind it. They feel the God of Christianity isn't strong enough to defend himself against those who have different opinions.

They don't realize that they have made God a small god, a personal god, a defenseless god, a silent god — and that's why they have to stand up and fight so viciously on his behalf. They also don't recognize that all the while, God is working in ways far beyond the understanding of the people who misuse and abuse God's commandments.

*God is working in ways far beyond the understanding of the people who misuse and abuse God's commandments.*

## ATTITUDES TO OVERCOME

Somebody rightly said that if you want to keep friends, don't discuss religion or politics. But in my position, I have to speak about religious teachings. It is just not possible to please everyone all the time. Truth cuts across the grain; it rarely goes the way people like to hear it. It didn't at the time of Christ, and it doesn't today.

Some associates of Jesus could not accept him in his day. They have reincarnated many times since. Some of them came into modern times. If you were to ask them, they would insist that, had they been alive in those days, they definitely would have recognized Jesus as the spiritual giant of the age.

The same people have come across the ECK Masters in many lifetimes. Out of ignorance, they have often turned their backs on these divine messengers of God. They wouldn't believe that either.

Eventually all these attitudes will be overcome through experience. Experience brings the awareness of Soul, which ultimately is love—the expression and the practice of love in everyday life.

## SMOKE ALARM

Protection sometimes comes to the ECKist through both the waking dream (a noticeable event that takes place in outer life) and the Golden-tongued Wisdom (when the voice of the Mahanta jumps out to impart spiritual insight, which can come in the words spoken by another person).

An initiate was sound asleep one night. All of a sudden her smoke alarm woke her with a loud peeping sound. She got up to see what was wrong and found that the noise was just a warning that the smoke alarm needed a new battery. She disconnected it and went back to bed, planning to replace the battery in the morning. She didn't realize it yet, but this was the first part of a waking dream.

Soon after that, she ran into a friend who had the ability to see events coming up in other people's lives. The woman was very distraught as she approached the ECKist. "I'm concerned about you," she said. "I see you as a small white cloud, and next to you is a black cloud, engulfing you."

Many others had dismissed this woman's warnings of impending danger. She was afraid that the ECKist wouldn't believe her either, and that's why she was so distraught. But this time she came to bring the Golden-tongued Wisdom.

The ECKist tried to figure out the meaning of her friend's vision. Was it significant spiritually? Or did it mean that something was going to happen to her physically? At this point she wasn't sure.

*Experience brings the awareness of Soul, which ultimately is love—the expression and the practice of love in everyday life.*

Later that day, the ECKist and her husband arrived home. She went into the kitchen, and as soon as she switched on the fluorescent light, there was a loud noise, a bright flash, and smoke all over the place. The bulb had burned out. The incident reminded her to replace the battery in the smoke alarm.

The next morning she went out and bought another fluorescent bulb. As soon as she brought it home, she installed it and flipped the switch to try it out. Once again there was a loud noise, bright flash, and smoke. She quickly turned off the switch; then she went to the fuse box and shut off all the electricity to the kitchen.

When her husband came home that evening, she said, "I think the ECK is trying to tell us something." He didn't take it too seriously, but he thought it would be a good idea to check out the light anyway.

He took the ceiling fixture apart and discovered that the entire interior was burned to a crisp. If the ECKist had simply turned off the switch in the kitchen rather than shutting off the power at the fuse box, they could have ended up with a major house fire. Her friend's prophecy about black smoke engulfing the little white cloud would have come true.

## WE ALWAYS GET WARNINGS

The Mahanta gave protection to the ECK initiate and her husband in three different ways. First there was the waking dream: her smoke-alarm battery sounded a warning to put her on the alert. Next came the Golden-tongued Wisdom: a friend brought a very specific verbal warning. Finally, she had another waking dream: the kitchen light burned out, signaling a true potential problem.

This experience is an example of the many ways

*The Mahanta gave protection to the ECK initiate and her husband in three different ways.*

protection can come into your life. In this case, several different elements were working at the same time. Three separate warnings were given. Had the woman ignored them, she might very well have been the victim of a bad fire.

When dangers like this come into your life, you too are given one, two, three, or even more warnings. Most people don't have the awareness to see when the Master is giving warnings for their protection.

## INTERCONNECTED WHEELS

I'm trying to help you develop your spiritual awareness, to bring you to the realization that all life is a series of interconnected wheels.

Through the *ECK Dream Discourses* and the Spiritual Exercises of ECK, I'm trying to help you develop your spiritual awareness, to bring you to the realization that all life is a series of interconnected wheels. Very little can happen to you that isn't known by you beforehand. All you have to do is learn to be aware.

This is not as easy as it sounds. It doesn't happen overnight; we don't go straight upward in our awareness. We may do very well for a while, then all of a sudden we go into a downward cycle. But there is no reason to get discouraged. Eventually the cycle takes a turn again, and we come back stronger in our awareness than we were at the last peak. This is how our awareness goes—up and down, up and down—hopefully always moving toward greater awareness.

## HERE IS HOLY GROUND

On the inner planes, just as out here, I sometimes see people doing things that don't make sense. They're off on a narrow path, and they don't know it. So I just watch.

Once I saw a crowd gathered in the foothills of a mountainous region on the inner planes. The people had come to see a band of pilgrims off on a long, dangerous journey up the mountain. The pilgrims' destination was a holy place, a sanctuary of wisdom many days' travel away. There they could get the wisdom that was not available to them in the present place.

The pilgrims set off on their journey, while the crowd applauded and cheered them on. "Look at them go," the people shouted, just as they would at a sporting event. "You guys are really something. Good luck to you and have a great time!"

The leader of the pilgrims stopped walking and turned to look back at the crowd. In a very stern voice he said to them, "You must meditate more."

He knew that these people were enjoying themselves immensely as they sent the pilgrims off on their long, hard journey. Why not? It was a lot more fun to applaud someone else than to join them on the journey.

But the leader took exception to this. Essentially his message was: We are holier than you; you should follow our example. Even if you don't come on this sacred pilgrimage, you should at least meditate more.

I stood in the crowd and watched the pilgrims go off on that long, difficult journey along winding mountain paths. I remembered another group that had gone on a similar pilgrimage years earlier. After several months, two stragglers came back and announced, "It wasn't there."

They had learned from their journey that wherever they walked was holy ground. What they were looking for was not a place. It was a state of consciousness.

*Heaven is not a place as much as it is your state of consciousness.*

## HEAVEN IS A STATE OF CONSCIOUSNESS

Heaven is not a place as much as it is your state of consciousness. This is where you go in your dreamland. You go to heaven, but you go there in a state of consciousness. Yet you wear a body, see other people, and participate in the activities there. So objectively, it is a place. But subjectively, in a spiritual way, it is a state of consciousness. It's not important what's there. What's important is what you learn from being there.

## DREAM DICTIONARY

One ECK initiate uses a technique to interpret his dreams that he calls a dream dictionary. In a section at the back of his dream journal, he keeps a list of the symbols that occur in his dreams.

During important times in my life, one of the dream symbols I used to see was a field with a regular-size baseball diamond. When everything on the field was aligned and in proper order—four bases evenly spaced, a pitcher, a batter, and two opposing teams—it meant that my life was in good order.

But sometimes the bases were at odd distances apart or the base path wasn't in a perfect square. Or the ball I'd hit might pop and blow feathers all over the place. Or I'd have to run into the woods to find first base. Second base might be closer in than usual; third base might be off in another direction entirely. In other words, everything about the game was wrong.

When I'd wake up after a dream like that, I'd often notice that something in my outer life wasn't going right. The sport had gone out of it. There wasn't any fun in it.

This was an indication for me to sit down and work out a plan to reorganize. In other words, I had to figure out how to get myself a real baseball field again—proper space between bases, correct number of players on each team, and so on.

## Your Dream Symbols

A dream dictionary can help you become familiar with your own dream symbols. Whether a bear, an eagle, or anything else, you'll know immediately what that particular symbol means to you.

Each symbol will have a unique meaning for each dreamer. This is where many books on dream symbology go wrong. They try to create a generic set of symbols to fit everybody, all the time, under every condition. It doesn't work that way.

As you create your own dream dictionary of symbols, record the date next to the meaning of each symbol so that you can keep track as the meaning changes. As you unfold, your dream symbols are going to take on different meanings, a fact generally not known by people who study dreams.

*A dream dictionary can help you become familiar with your own dream symbols.*

*ECK Springtime Seminar, San Diego, California, Saturday, March 25, 1989*

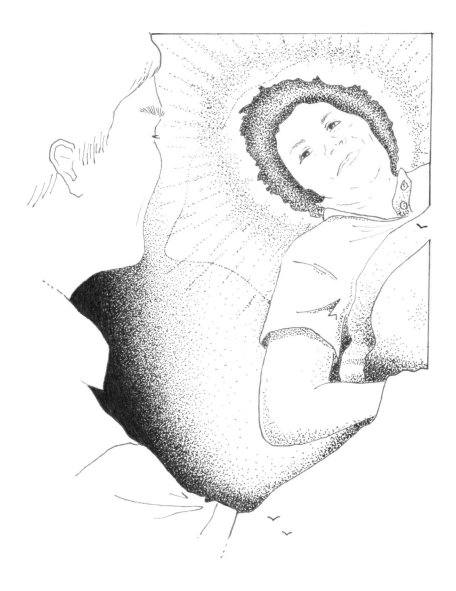

They held hands as she spoke, and he was able to perceive the living truth of the Light and Sound of God that she had experienced in the other worlds.

# 8

# ECK, EASTER, AND RESURRECTION

*E*aster was always a happy day for me as I was growing up. The best part about it was that it followed Lent. Everything that happened during Lent seemed depressing, especially having to attend the Wednesday-night services in our country church.

It's not a pleasant experience for a little kid to have to get dressed up, go out to the cold car in the worst part of winter, and drive to church with the family. The service lasted for over an hour. As a boy of four or five, I would get so tired that my eyes would roll back in my head. Just as I was about to drop off, there would be a poke in the ribs from Mother, warning me to stay awake and catch everything that was being said.

The weather reports for those years may not support my memory of Easter as always being a day of sunshine, but it sure seemed that way. Maybe knowing that we were done with Lent was enough to brighten the day.

## WHAT DOES YOUR RELIGION DO FOR YOU?

Certain things that I have found to be truth sometimes offend people who believe differently. Yet,

*Certain things that I have found to be truth sometimes offend people who believe differently.*

*The true value of a religion is what it does for the people who are in it.*

all paths are valid. The theology of a path is not really that important, except perhaps to the clergy. The true value of a religion is what it does for the people who are in it.

Whether you are in Eckankar, one of the Christian denominations, Buddhism, or anything else, the question is the same: Is the path helping you to become a more spiritual being? Does this show in your everyday life? These are the important points.

## SPIRITUAL SERVICE

Sometimes I pound on the walls of theology where the differences between ECK and Christianity, for instance, are most apparent. But just because we are different, it doesn't mean that we can't allow other people to believe the way they wish.

*The outer path of Eckankar exists, in part, to explain the twin aspects of Light and Sound to people who encounter them.*

The outer path of Eckankar exists, in part, to explain the twin aspects of Light and Sound to people who encounter them. This is a major spiritual service to people who need an explanation for the things of God that are unknown to their own religious leaders.

## NO NEED FOR REDEMPTION

In a conversation with someone last night, I got to thinking about the differences between ECK and Christianity. I said, "The entire Christian religion seems to be built upon the foundation of original sin."

In Christianity, original sin means the spiritual depravity that a person supposedly takes on as he is born because of Adam's fall, and there is nothing you can do about it. You don't even have a chance to find out if you are going to be good or bad; the second you are born, you are spiritually depraved. Your only hope is to find baptism, believe in Christ, and be saved.

I once tried to trace back the meaning of birth

under the conditions of original sin. The theology dictates that as soon as you enter this life through a woman's body, you are automatically spiritually corrupt. This is the original sin that damns the Christian to hell until he accepts Christ and is saved.

If you take away the piece of the puzzle called original sin, what would be left of the picture? There would be no need for redemption, which means there would be no need for Christ. And if you take away Christ, then there isn't any Christianity.

Theology isn't necessarily the spiritual element in a teaching. Often the religious leaders consider theology the lifeblood of a religion, but it's not. It's something the leaders like to play around with so they can convince the followers that their religion is more valid than others.

People do the best they can in their religion without really understanding the reasons for what they are doing. They muddle their way from the incomprehensible reason for birth to the incomprehensible reason for death, and assume if they do everything they were taught to do, they'll go to their reward in heaven.

*If you take away the piece of the puzzle called original sin, what would be left of the picture?*

## WHAT DID SOUL LEARN?

With original sin as the very core of such a teaching, there really is no reason for Soul to come into the human body. One of the defects of Christian theology is that it doesn't give a reason for birth, except as a way to get out of this life.

So what do you do in the meantime? Much is made of the eleventh-hour confession. This means you can live a really rotten life until the very last minute. Then you can call in a priest, confess your sins, and be received into heaven. If this is the case, then what did you learn from this whole experience?

Actually, the ECKist, the Christian, the Buddhist,

and everybody else does learn something. The real learning goes beyond the theology of most religions.

## PRACTICING LOVE

These are pretty pointed statements, but I feel they have to be made. I also want to point out that Christianity is a good garden for the spiritual growth of many people. These are the people who either don't know the theology, or don't let the theology of Christianity limit them. They just live a life of love.

In ECK and in life, we learn that love and understanding can erase anger, intolerance, and other perversions of the mind. Those who practice love and understanding will gain more out of this life than some of their religious leaders. A leader may know the theology of his particular religion by heart, but he may not know the meaning of love.

This is the difference between the theology and the practice of one's religion. The practice, of course, has to be founded on love.

## WE HAVE LIVED BEFORE

In ECK we don't begin with original sin; we look at life quite differently. Many Christians believe that life begins at birth—as if the creation of Soul takes place at the birth of the human body—and ends at death, and then continues on in heaven.

In ECK we learn, sometimes through past-life experiences in the dream state, that we have lived more than just one life. We have lived thousands of lives. In each life we gather talents, tools, and lessons which help in our spiritual unfoldment in subsequent lifetimes, including this one. Christianity's arena is limited to this one physical lifetime; in ECK we gain a broader vision. We recognize that Soul enters many different bodies throughout Its journey in the lower worlds.

The ECKist learns that the reason he is reborn again and again is to learn how to love, to overcome those traits which prevent him or her from becoming a Co-worker with God. In each life we learn a little bit more. There is, of course, the grace of God which brings us to the Light and Sound and to the Mahanta; but at the same time, there is just as much effort required on our part.

In Christianity, it's usually just grace, even at the eleventh hour. It's something that either does or doesn't come to you, and if it comes, then you're fine.

## SELF-RESPONSIBILITY VERSUS FAITH

A broader understanding of how life really works comes with the recognition that self-responsibility is more important than faith. When a person has a certain illness, we learn it's probably a condition brought forward from a past life. The individual chose to come into this life with that condition in order to learn a spiritual lesson. Faith is fine, but the belief that someone else is going to pay your debts is untrue.

In Christianity, there is no real understanding of why certain things happen. "Why do children die?" they ask. "It's not fair." The questions arise because the theology isn't broad enough to encompass the spiritual truth of God.

When an ECKist makes a mistake spiritually in his day-to-day living, it creates karma, a debt. When a Christian makes such a mistake, it's called sin. How is sin taken care of? Christians are told that Jesus, the redeemer, takes care of it. Believe in him and ye shall be saved—this sort of thing.

In ECK we realize that, in one way or another,

*The ECKist learns that the reason he is reborn again and again is to learn how to love, to overcome those traits which prevent him or her from becoming a Co-worker with God.*

the person who created the debt is going to have to repay it. Somehow it is going to have to be balanced in his own ledger book.

Faith is a starting point on the path to God. But faith in ECK is based on knowledge, and knowledge is based on experience. Experience brings awareness, and awareness leads to a greater trust in ECK.

## POWER OF HU

Often I get letters from the initiates in Africa, and their faith in ECK is strong.

An ECKist in Africa came home from work and went into the kitchen to make himself a quick lunch. No one else was home. He lit a fire on the two-burner stove which was set on a table.

Previously, his wife had complained about their kerosene stove. "There are some leaks in it," she had told him. "It's getting very dangerous to cook food on that stove." But he was in such a hurry to have lunch that he forgot about the defect in the stove.

After he lit the stove, he bent down to get a knife from a container underneath the table. As he stood up, he saw that the entire stove and the top of the table were engulfed in flames. He quickly grabbed an aluminum washbasin and put it over the stove. *I'll snuff out the fire through lack of oxygen,* he thought. *To throw water on it will just spread the fire.*

He then took other pots and pans and tried to cover the flames wherever they popped up. He tried everything, but nothing worked; the fire kept spreading.

Suddenly, a divine feeling of the heavenly sound of HU came into his mind, and with it came the understanding that he should chant. In a low, strong voice, he began to chant "HU-U-U-U-U," while hold-

*Faith is a starting point on the path to God.*

*The heavenly sound of HU came into his mind, and with it came the understanding that he should chant.*

ing his hand over the fire.

Here in America most people would say, "Watch out, you'll burn your hand!" But this was his home, and he was at risk of losing it. He said he felt like Moses at the Red Sea, raising his hand to make things work right.

As he held his hand over the flames, he heard a clicking sound, as if the grip of some invisible being had let go. Seconds later, the fire went out.

The stove was destroyed, and the entire tabletop was burned; but he had saved his home. And in the process, he had learned something very important: The sound of HU came to him just when he needed it, and he had saved his home through chanting HU, the love song to God.

## FAITH AS A STARTING POINT

The people in countries far from America learn to rely more on the Inner Master. They simply don't get to see the Outer Master very often.

*The people in countries far from America learn to rely more on the Inner Master.*

Their connection with the Inner Master becomes so strong that they can do things that we, living in a more scientific society, would consider foolish to attempt. We likely wouldn't even know how to go about it. We have come to rely so strongly upon outer forces that we would probably go for the fire extinguisher and hope that it still worked.

In the Christian Bible (Matthew 9:29), Christ is quoted as saying, "According to your faith be it unto you." This is the kind of faith we develop in ECK as a starting point. But from here we go on—to knowledge, experience, and an awareness of the workings of the Holy Spirit, the ECK. We begin to have experiences with the Light and Sound of God, and thus we develop a greater understanding of the spiritual laws of life. Knowing these laws, we can then make our own life easier.

## PROOF OF THE LIGHT AND SOUND

An atheist and his wife were friends with two Higher Initiates in ECK. Though they were very close, the atheist always thought that the ECKists were making up the things they said about the Light and Sound of God. He didn't understand that when ECKists speak about the Light and Sound, we mean a very real experience.

During contemplation, and sometimes with our eyes wide open, we actually see the Blue Light. We can see a white light, a green or yellow light, or sparkling blue lights. The Blue Light always indicates the presence of the Mahanta. It means his protection is with you. It is living proof of the statement *I am always with you.*

*The Sound can actually be heard. It comes in a number of different ways.*

The Sound can actually be heard. It comes in a number of different ways. Sometimes It sounds like the high humming of a generator or like a kitchen blender heard at a distance. Other times It comes as the sound of a bird singing or a flute being played in the same room with you—very real sounds.

The Light and Sound are the vision and the music of God. Each time they come to you, you are lifted in spiritual consciousness.

The atheist didn't really believe the ECKists when they spoke of the Light and Sound. But it happened that his wife contracted a terminal illness, and over a period of time, she grew weaker and weaker.

One night the wife was lying in her bed at home. As the husband held her hand, he felt the life force leave her, and he was sure that she had died.

But then the life force returned. His wife opened

her eyes and said to him, "I have been to a place of light, of such love, where I had perceptions that I have never known before." They held hands as she spoke, and he was able to perceive the living truth of the Light and Sound of God that she had experienced in the other worlds.

She lived for a short time after that, and then she translated. But at various times since her death, he has felt her near, always with a feeling of love. It was as if she had come into this life, at least in part, to teach him about the Light and Sound of God. Something had happened to him in a past life to sour him on the idea of a divine being. In this life, the effect was undone through the love of his wife and through the experience she was able to share with him.

## RESURRECTION

The fifteen-year-old son of an African ECKist stepped on something, sustained a wound to his foot, then died of tetanus. The man very much wanted to meet with his son in the other worlds.

One day he went into contemplation and began to chant HU. Through Soul Travel, he went in the Soul body and met with his son. They greeted each other with love and joy, and then the father asked the questions that had been weighing on his mind.

"Where did you hurt yourself?" he asked his son. "What did you step on that caused the tetanus?"

"It happened in the passageway that leads to the kitchen," the son said. "In the corner is a nail."

When the father returned from contemplation, he quickly got out of bed and went to the kitchen passageway. There in the corner he found the nail that his son had stepped on. It was out of the way, not where they normally walked, but his son had just

*Through Soul Travel, he went in the Soul body and met with his son.*

happened to step on it.

Because of his contemplation, the man was able to pull the nail out and make sure that no one else's health would be endangered. And even though he went through the anguish of his son's translation, he was able to find proof that his son had been "resurrected."

To most people, *resurrection* means the extinguishing of life, and then a rising again of the body. This is not true. Life is never extinguished; it continues on. Life is a steady stream of consciousness. When I speak of the man seeing that his son had been resurrected, I mean it as a continuation of the son's life in another body, on another plane. Through Soul Travel, the father was able to see this and to speak with his son on the inner planes.

*Life is never extinguished; it continues on. Life is a steady stream of consciousness.*

## Live Life Here

You can meet with departed relatives in the dream state if there is a strong love bond, but eventually you give that up. You come to realize that you have other interests to pursue in your current life here on the physical plane.

No one should make the mistake of thinking that we should spend this life with our heads in the clouds, hoping and living for the moment of translation. Life is life, whether it's here on the physical plane or in the other worlds. Each plane has something to teach, and on each plane we have the opportunity to move forward spiritually.

## Chatter

An ECK initiate who volunteers as a hospice worker made arrangements to meet with a terminally ill patient. The patient had a malignancy in his brain and was not expected to live much longer. It was just a matter of time.

The hospice volunteer visited the man twice a week for two hours. He learned that the patient had been talkative before his illness, but now he went on nonstop, chattering like a blue jay from the beginning of their meeting until the end. The ECKist never had a chance to give him any kind of spiritual help, to tell him about the HU. He would leave thoroughly exhausted.

One night in contemplation he asked the Mahanta, "Is there anything you can do about that man's constant chatter?"

"You only have to listen to his chatter for two hours, twice a week," the Master said to him. "I have to listen to you nearly twenty-four hours a day."

The answer came as quite a surprise to the ECKist, but he caught the message.

He works his regular job during the evening on the swing shift, gets home about one o'clock in the morning, and generally goes to bed about 3:00 a.m. One night he suddenly felt so tired that he couldn't stay awake. It wasn't his usual bedtime yet, but he headed for the bed and fell right to sleep.

During the night the Mahanta took him out in the Soul body, where he was able to view the translation of the terminal patient. The first thing the ECKist noticed was the look of happy surprise on the face of this man, who had been so anxious about his impending translation.

*During the night the Mahanta took him out in the Soul body, where he was able to view the translation of the terminal patient.*

The ECKist now realized why the man had talked so much. He was so afraid that he hadn't known where to turn for help. The help was right there, but because the man talked so much, the ECKist never got a chance to tell him about HU. When the man had to face the moment of his translation, it was with wonder and surprise at how easy it was to go into the next cycle of life. It was a very natural transition.

## MATERIAL OR SPIRITUAL RELIGION?

At one point before he left earth, Christ told his disciples that some of them would see the Kingdom of God in this lifetime. He was trying to tell them about the continuation of the spiritual body.

The resurrection is when one leaves the physical body and just steps into the other worlds in full consciousness. The followers of Christianity have misunderstood this teaching. They have turned it into a physical, or material, resurrection. This, to me, is the sign of a material, instead of a spiritual, religion.

A religion provides an outer structure or fabric. Within this structure people have the right to feel free to live a spiritually good life or to live a negative life. The religion is just a framework; it is meaningless in the sense that anything on earth is temporal.

Even the outer teachings of ECK are temporal. The Bible, a book that has been mistranslated and misinterpreted over the years, is temporal. But Christians have made it into the living word. Yet, the only true element that remains today—though often disregarded—is the teaching that people should love each other, even those who do not love them.

*Taking responsibility for one's own actions is deeply embedded in the teachings of Eckankar.*

## MORE THAN GETTING BY

Taking responsibility for one's own actions is deeply embedded in the teachings of Eckankar. This is because the curtain between cause and effect is lifted for the ECK initiate. He sees very quickly how his actions cause situations to occur in his life.

People not in ECK sometimes get by with things

for a couple of weeks, months, or years—or even a couple of lifetimes. They don't believe they live more than one lifetime, so when their actions finally return to them, they miss the lesson.

And it really doesn't matter. Whether or not one understands about all those lifetimes is not important. What really matters is this: Does the person express divine love in his everyday life? Some do, some don't—whether ECKists, Christians, or anyone else.

*Every day is a lesson in humility, because humility brings us to love.*

None of us has anything to be vain about. Every day is a lesson in humility, because humility brings us to love. We are being taught to look for the divine nature that exists in other people as well as in ourself. This is what Christ tried to tell his followers when he said, "Love your neighbor as yourself."

If you can recognize your own divinity, why not recognize your neighbor's? Then you can love him. And while you're at it, don't forget to love yourself.

Original sin has a funny effect on those who take the theology of Christianity too seriously. They constantly feel the weight of the original sin and think of themselves as poor lost sheep. So to them I would say, Don't take the theology too seriously. Live the life of Christianity with love, and you will make great strides in the spiritual path.

## How Do You Spend Your Last Days?

An initiate in WestAfrica learned about the truth of the ECK teachings through an experience he had with his friend, Lewis, who is also an ECKist.

One day Lewis, a twenty-five-year-old bachelor, came to the ECKist and said, "I just got a very good job with an oil-drilling company. I'll be working on a sophisticated computer."

An interesting point is that out of the hundred applicants for that position, Lewis was the only one who did not have a degree in higher education. But he did have the quiet certainty that he could do the job. He went on to tell his friend the rest of the story.

One of the members of the review panel had tried to dissuade the others from considering Lewis. "Since he doesn't have a higher degree, we ought to disqualify him."

But another review panel member, an American, said, "No, let's give him a fair chance. He's here, he's had three months of training on another computer, and he has shown some expertise. Let him take the test." The rest of the review panel finally agreed to let Lewis take the test. Each candidate was given fifteen minutes to work out a series of complex problems. Lewis got busy, worked everything out, finished before the fifteen minutes was up, and ended up with higher marks than any of the other candidates.

When it was announced that he had been chosen for the job, one of the other candidates came over to chat with him. She said, "Throughout this entire review, I have noticed how calm and confident you were; you have a happy countenance." Lewis responded pleasantly, but he didn't elaborate.

*Then he said, "I had a dream, and I'm going to translate very soon."*

Later, after he finished telling all this to his ECKist friend, he said, "I have two more things to tell you. First, the reason I did so well on the computer is that the Mahanta has been teaching me how to run it on the inner planes. When it came time to take the test on the physical computer, it was very easy."

Then he said, "The second thing I have to tell you is that I had a dream, and I'm going to translate very soon."

The ECK initiate just about fell over. He couldn't

believe that he was hearing these words from Lewis, a young man standing at the threshold of a promising and brilliant career. "You must have mistaken the meaning of your dream," he said.

Lewis shook his head. "No, I went back to the Inner Master and asked for verification. The Master said that the dream was true, that I would translate in six weeks."

But Lewis had some things to take care of that would require more than six weeks. "Could the timing be postponed for a little while?" he asked the Master. "Of course it can," the Inner Master said. And so a postponement was arranged.

Lewis began to get his outer affairs in order. For the first week or two after the dream, he wore a worried look on his face. He had become attached to his human body, to his friends, and to his life in general. And, for a brief time, the teachings from his Christian past came creeping in. But the worry soon passed, and once again he was able to show his confidence, his loving nature, and his good will.

One day he said to his ECKist friend, "The company has decided to send me to the United States for additional training. I'm supposed to leave within the next month." The date of the trip was scheduled very close to the predicted date of his translation.

A few days later the two ECKists went to a lawyer so that Lewis could have his will prepared. Lewis then bought some gifts and took them back to his hometown. He confided his dream to a few close ECK friends, gave them his gifts, and had a very happy supper with them.

That night he went to bed, and very quietly during the night, he translated. His health condition was unknown to most people, and so his death

*That night he went to bed, and very quietly during the night, he translated.*

was totally unexpected to all but a few. But he had been given time to prepare, and he used it to give his love to other people.

The ECKist who remained in the physical body learned many things about the truth of ECK, the ECK-Vidya, the dream state, and the spiritual laws of the Holy Spirit. The sharing of the experience was Lewis's gift to him.

## CONTINUITY OF LIFE

*Translation is a fact of life. It's the natural step into the other worlds. In ECK we recognize it as a continuation of life.*

Translation is a fact of life. It's the natural step into the other worlds. In ECK we recognize it as a continuation of life.

Translation occurs on the inner planes too. Many of you believe we go from the physical body to one of the other planes and there we stay. But at some point, the people who reside on the inner planes also move on to higher planes in the spiritual worlds. Their translation is much the same as moving from the Physical to the Astral Plane.

For a while I had daily meetings with an elderly man on the inner planes. He reminded me of Joseph Campbell, the noted mythologist, who translated a couple of years ago. About eighty years old in terms of earth years, the gentleman had a certain presence and bearing about him.

He was very interested in ECK. He especially wanted to know more about HU and the Light and Sound. In our meetings, we would sit and talk about these things. We never exchanged names—that would have brought an unneeded element into the picture, perhaps smudging the high spiritual content of the discussion.

One day I arrived at an office building on the inner planes, where I was to talk to some businessmen about ECK. I went into a reception area. A lavish buffet had been set up. It looked as if other guests were about to arrive.

At the far end of the room was a conference table. Ten members of the board of directors sat around the table with surprised looks on their faces. They had just found out about the translation of one of their fellow directors, a Mr. Caruthers. Nobody knew his background, except that he had always given freely of his wisdom and knowledge. They were awed at learning that he had translated; no one knew what to make of it.

As we all talked, a thought suddenly struck me. "Do you have a picture of Mr. Caruthers?" I asked them. They looked around until someone found a photograph that had been taken about twenty years earlier. It was a much younger version of the man I secretly called Mr. HU.

He and I had met here because he needed to hear about the HU and the Light and Sound. These were the tools he needed in order to progress to the next higher spiritual level.

You, as ECKists, are very special messengers of the Mahanta. You take the ECK teachings out into the world not only to teach, but also to learn the spiritual truths of the Light and Sound.

On your journey home, I am always with you.

*You take the ECK teachings out into the world not only to teach, but also to learn the spiritual truths of the Light and Sound.*

*ECK Springtime Seminar, San Diego, California, Sunday, March 26, 1989*

*Field of Dreams* is not really a story about baseball; it's about unfulfilled dreams. The point of the ECK teachings is to learn that heaven is wherever dwells a person with a spiritualized consciousness.

# 9
# FIELD OF DREAMS

he ECK seminars are opportunities for the performers in ECK to express the Light and Sound of God in their own particular way, with their particular talents. I often wish that people could recognize the benefits and opportunities for spiritual growth that await them at the ECK seminars. The seminar sites are chosen very carefully.

## A SPIRITUAL JOURNEY

In ECK we recognize that life is a very real dream world. Everywhere we go is a spiritual occasion, whether it's to the seminar or to the local attractions that have nothing to do with the ECK functions. The Holy Spirit is always working to give you understanding and bring you knowledge about life and living. The entire trip, from the time you leave home until the time you return home, is a spiritual journey of a special kind.

Not everyone is able to travel to these seminars, and some are only able to attend one every year or two. But whenever you can come, the occasion is special. The Holy Spirit is always working with

*In ECK we recognize that life is a very real dream world.*

you to show you something about the laws of the cosmic order.

In a glitzy society like ours, people sometimes take the opportunities of the ECK seminars for granted. They say, "Oh, I went to the one in Anaheim, or San Diego, or Orlando, or New York City." They feel their experience begins and ends with that. They equate the entire experience with the outer circumstances. Not knowingly, of course; but this is often what people do.

Most of what happens to an ECK student at the seminars takes place on the invisible, subjective side. But the hidden forces of life also become more objective during these times, when the scenery and experiences are new. The adventure of travel brings you out of the routine of everyday living—work and all the other things that make up your usual week.

Routine can shut down the guidance of the Holy Spirit. The guidance is always there, but all too often one allows routine to shut out the wisdom of the ages. I guess you could say it's a matter of consciousness— or unconsciousness.

*The guidance is always there, but often one allows routine to shut out the wisdom of the ages.*

## COMPLETING SOMETHING WITHIN

The individuals who participated in *Show Time Two: Destination Now,* the play you saw last night, went through a period of rapid spiritual growth. One actor said, "I'll never do another play unless I have a completed script in my hand." One person involved in the rewriting said, "I don't ever want to write another play." There were some difficult times, but perhaps the play itself was an anticlimax to what really occurred.

At rocky intervals along the way, I wondered how they were going to pull it off. I crossed my fingers and hoped for the best. But I was betting on the creative skills of the ECKists—those who work backstage, the writers, actors, and so on. I knew they would make it.

I'm trying to allow people who love the ECK the opportunity to express their talents. In this way they can fine-tune their skills in music, acting, writing, or any of the other areas that help a project reach fulfillment. As individuals work together to bring something to a conclusion, they complete something within themselves. They realize that no matter how big or difficult an enterprise may seem, by doing their part and working in harmony, there is a way to get through it.

*They realize that no matter how big or difficult an enterprise may seem, by doing their part and working in harmony, there is a way to get through it.*

## FIELD OF DREAMS

Recently my wife and I went to our annual movie and got our annual box of theater popcorn. I noticed that the popcorn is almost as expensive as the tickets. We wanted to see *Field of Dreams*. Some time ago I had written an article about the incident on which the movie is based.

In the 1919 World Series, "Shoeless Joe" Jackson and seven other members of the Chicago White Sox were involved in a scandal. The result: the eight players were barred forever from playing baseball. Because of ignorance, they were not allowed to complete a cycle, to reach a conclusion in a career they dearly loved.

These players were among the best in baseball at the time. But the movie is not really a story about baseball; it's about unfulfilled dreams.

Kevin Costner plays the main character, Ray Kinsella, a protester from the 1960s who married a girl from Iowa. The story begins shortly after they move to Iowa and buy a farm, where they live with their young daughter.

In an early scene where Ray is walking through his cornfield, I thought about something that the farmers say: "If it's knee-high by July, it's on schedule." The movie corn was about a month and a half beyond knee-high. With my background in farming, I look for these things.

"Judging by the height of the corn, it looks like they shot this scene in August," I told my wife.

"Uh-huh," she said and ate some popcorn, which meant, Be quiet, I can't hear the movie.

Anyway, Ray is in the cornfield and his wife and daughter are sitting on the porch swing of their home, about a baseball throw from where's he's walking. All of a sudden he hears a voice, speaking to him in a whisper. It says, *If you build it, he will come.*

Ray looks around but continues on. Then he hears the voice a second time.

"What was that?" he calls out to his wife.

"We didn't hear anything," she says.

He walks a little farther through the corn, and the voice whispers to him a third time: *If you build it, he will come.*

Ray is a hard-eyed realist from the sixties, and he doesn't know what to make of this. But the next time he's in the cornfield and the voice comes, he has a vision of a baseball field and a ballplayer he recognizes as "Shoeless Joe" Jackson.

He tells his wife that he thinks he is supposed to build a ball field so that Shoeless Joe can get to come back and play baseball. She knows they are in danger of losing the farm if they can't make the mortgage payments, but when he explains how much it means to him, she finally agrees. "If you really feel you should do this, then you should do it."

The neighbors watch with great curiosity as Ray

begins to plow under his major crop and build a baseball diamond. Finally he completes it and waits.

One evening, while he and his wife are trying to figure out how they can keep the farm and the ball field, too, Shoeless Joe comes. He and Ray toss the ball around for a while, and then Shoeless Joe says, "There are others, you know. . . . It would really mean a lot to them." Ray, of course, says yes.

As he's leaving for the night, Shoeless Joe turns to Ray and says, "Hey, is this heaven?"

"No," Ray says. "It's Iowa."

Shoeless Joe returns the next day with the seven other suspended team members. While Ray and his daughter are watching them practice, he learns an interesting thing about this baseball field. Although he and his wife and daughter can see the baseball players, no one else can. Only when the magic of the inner vision is opened can a person see it.

## WHAT IS A SAINT?

The point of the ECK teachings is to learn that heaven is found wherever a person with a spiritualized consciousness dwells. Heaven is the ground you walk on, and the one who can see it is a holy person.

*Heaven is found wherever a person with a spiritualized consciousness dwells.*

This stretches the usual definition of a saint. Most people think of a saint as a religious person who has lived a life of hardship, perhaps spent in contemplation or working among the poor. Short of Mother Teresa, there are very few people living today whom the general population would consider to be saints.

My definition of a saint is a person who recognizes the present moment as a holy, sacred occasion in which he or she is working and responding with the Holy Spirit. A saint is one who knows the holiness of the moment, here and now. Therefore, by definition, a saint is a happy individual, no matter what he or she is doing.

## THE HOLINESS OF THE MOMENT

I'm always struck by people who do their jobs well. In the restaurant where I had dinner the last few evenings, I began to observe a young woman who worked there in different capacities. One night she was working as the hostess, seating the customers. More than just leading them to their table, she seemed sincerely interested in making sure they were comfortable.

The next night found her behind the buffet serving line. There were other young women helping out back there, but they were too busy discussing their social life to pay attention to the customers. This particular young lady took time to explain the different foods to each customer. She went through a lot of trouble to make sure that they understood what they would be getting.

I look for people like this, who enjoy what they're doing. No matter what it is, they are living fully in the moment. Some work as hair stylists who, instead of complaining about tangled hair, enjoy turning it into something beautiful. In the eyes of the expert stylist who cares about what he or she is doing, tangled hair brings all kinds of possibilities just waiting to be created.

*A person who lives in the holiness of the moment is always looking for the potential in whatever they happen to be doing.*

A person who lives in the holiness of the moment is always looking for the potential in whatever they happen to be doing. They are always looking for ways to make everything around them better. These are people who will always take that extra step and do more than anyone else around them. They will go out of their way to do whatever is required to be of service to others.

I watch for these individuals and try to talk with them occasionally. I like to find out how they got to where they are now, what they're looking for in their work, and things of this nature. I like to talk with them because they're good company.

## EASE HIS PAIN

Shoeless Joe and his seven teammates would later bring other players to the field, enough to make up two teams so that they could play a real ball game. But before that, Ray hears the voice again. This time it whispers to him, *"Ease his pain."*

A series of events leads Ray to a reclusive author who in his youth had expressed a love for baseball. He went on to become an influential activist in the sixties, his interest in baseball long forgotten. Ray knew he had to get him to come to a ball game.

He has a very difficult time convincing the writer that this is all he wants. A powerful voice for the civil-rights and antiwar movements of the sixties, the writer had long since grown disenchanted. He now earns his living writing computer programs for children. "I don't have any answers for you," he tells Ray. "I don't do causes anymore."

Ray finally does convince the man to come with him to a baseball game, but I won't tell you how the story proceeds from there. It's the kind of movie that will be around for years to come. *Field of Dreams* is about a place where people can come to realize the dreams that seem to have disappeared into the past.

*Field of Dreams is about a place where people can come to realize the dreams that seem to have disappeared into the past.*

## CURVEBALL

I used to enjoy baseball very much. As a college freshman I had a roommate who actually knew how to throw a curveball. "The ball curved," I said the first time I saw him do it. "What did it? Was it the wind?"

"No," he said. "I threw a curve."

That really fascinated me. *If he can curve it,* I thought, *so can I.* So I began to practice my throws over and over, until I found that I could make the ball do marvelous things. It got to the point where all I wanted to do was throw the ball. We all have our own little things that make life worth living.

## BEING CONSCIOUS

An individual went to a shopping mall with his wife and a friend. As they walked down the main corridor, he pointed out to his friend how every so often a person would leave the mainstream to go into a shop here, another would go into a shop there, and so on. People in the crowd kept moving back and forth, leaving the mainstream as their attention drew them to a particular shop and then returning to the mainstream.

This is very much like life in general. As part of humanity, we move in and out of the shops in this life just as we have moved through past lives. In every life, each of us has gone off into our own little shop, sometimes to become weavers or sailors or artists.

Each profession is like a shop in a mall—it's the place where our interests and attention draw us. We spend a certain amount of time in each shop, in each lifetime, learning things, completely absorbed in the spiritual moment, except that we usually do it unconsciously.

*Whatever we do, we do it consciously.*

The whole point of the ECK teachings is that whatever we do, we do it consciously. We should be aware that we are leaving the crowd for a moment to shop where we want to. When we've had our fill of that shop, we can walk out and consciously rejoin the group of people moving in the corridor.

As the individual was explaining his ideas about humanity and shopping malls, his wife suddenly disappeared into a dress shop. "See that," he said to his friend. "She's gone. She's lost in her world, lost in her shop."

"That's pretty wild," the friend said, "but I see what you mean. People get lost and disappear into their own world. And while they're in that world, their atoms come more alive, because they're doing something they really want to do."

The first man agreed and was about to expound further, but as they walked past a camera shop, his friend veered off to the right. He then disappeared into the camera shop and got totally absorbed in examining the different types of cameras and lenses.

The man who was making these profound observations about humanity and shopping malls had no use for dresses or cameras. *My wife and friend are both lost in their own little worlds,* he thought. He felt very smug as he continued down the mall by himself, until he saw a hardware store. Without another thought, he headed for the store and immediately got lost in the world of drills and saws and other tools.

Minutes later, or maybe it was hours later, he felt a tap on his shoulder and heard his wife say, "Are you lost?" He realized then that his smug words had come right back at him.

## In Our Own Fields

All too often, before ECK, we have let other people lead us into the shops where they wanted to go. We thought we had to go with them just because they told us to.

I have always found it difficult to go into a dress

*All too often, before ECK, we have let other people lead us into the shops where they wanted to go.*

shop with my wife. Other men describe symptoms very similar to mine: nausea, dizzy spells, and severe disorientation that strikes on the spot.

Have you ever noticed that there are usually benches right outside the dress shops in malls? More often than not, these benches are filled with husbands, just sitting there waiting, like dogs on a leash. A few times I've been tempted to go up to one of them and say, "Don't you know you could be free? You could go to the hardware store!" But I guess that approach could lead to another set of problems.

With a little experience in marriage, you work out certain rules that suit both parties. My wife seldom goes shopping, but we have agreed that when she goes into a dress shop, I'll go off somewhere else. When we're both finished, we'll meet on neutral ground, some place we can both appreciate — like a restaurant.

I used to think I was being a good, patient husband when I went along to help her select an outfit. I would point to the rack and say, "There's a good dress. Take it. Let's go." I only meant to help — and get out of there as quickly as possible.

One time, as soon as we stepped into the dress shop, I began to feel dizzy and nauseated. At the front were two mannequins on a pedestal, observing the store. While my wife went off to search through the racks, I sat down on the base of the pedestal and just kind of crumpled up there. Worn and weary, I was sort of hanging on to the mannequins' feet so that I wouldn't slip to the floor.

Finally I staggered over to my wife. "I've just got to get out of here," I gasped, certain that she wouldn't understand.

"Well, go ahead," she said.

So I found that the agony was of my own making. All I'd had to do was say, as a courtesy, "I'll wait outside," meaning, so you won't have to look for me on the floor.

If we realize that our field of dreams is not the same as someone else's, we'll get along better with that person. This can be very difficult to learn.

## THE MEANING OF INNER EXPERIENCES

When I wake up in the morning, I sometimes lie there and think about the experiences that have just occurred on the inner planes. Many of them are pleasant, others are interesting and educational, and a few are frightening. But all together, I see them as actual experiences which occur on the inner planes.

If I'm going through a particular problem in my outer life, I might try to use dream experiences to extract the meaning of that problem. An inner experience can give us an insight into our outer experience. The dream becomes like a play with hidden meaning, which gives us a clue about the outcome of our outer life.

From this level, I look at an inner experience for symbols. I know the experience was real, but I'll strain to dig out the symbology that will help me understand what to do to make my physical life work better. I do that sometimes.

Most of the time I just accept the inner experiences at face value. Though my position in the past has been that dreams are in some way a reflection of our daily life, and our daily life is a reflection of the inner life, I'm now taking you a little bit further. You are going to find—and many of you have—that the experiences in the outer and inner worlds can be completely different. When this happens, don't strain

*If we realize that our field of dreams is not the same as someone else's, we'll get along better with that person.*

*An inner experience can give us an insight into our outer experience.*

yourself looking for a meaning to tie them together. Just accept it.

## ROLE OF DREAMS

What you are doing is living, moving, and acting in consciousness. Before the time that you remembered dreams or had any interest in your inner life, you thought dreams were flighty, unreal figments of the imagination, better kept to yourself. Why? Because people might laugh if you took your dreams seriously.

In some past cultures, dreams have played an important role in the complete life of the individual. In our present culture, dreams have been put in the background. This is simply because most of the leaders in psychology and various religions don't understand what really happens during dreams. It is not all symbology.

A few people have come up with some useful interpretations to explain how this dream symbolizes that occurrence in your daily life. There is nothing wrong with this. But they do not have the awareness to tell the dreamer, "Your inner life is a real life." Nor do they know how to lead the dreamer through the area of broken memories.

There are times when the dream memories may be disjointed and piecemeal, so that the dreamer believes there is no reality to his inner world. But you can work through it. Through the Spiritual Exercises of ECK, you can come to a better understanding of who you are and what your dreams mean.

*Through the Spiritual Exercises of ECK, you can come to a better understanding of who you are and what your dreams mean.*

## DISNEY-WORLD GUIDE

Some ECK initiates have experiences on the inner planes where they are helping a person find someone else. They are able to do this in full consciousness. In the past, the dreamer had had the opportunity to travel through the mazes of a particular region—on the Astral or Causal Plane, sometimes on the Mental Plane—and he or she knows the territory.

A person who lives in Orlando or who has traveled to Disney World several times can tell you, from firsthand experience, the best time to avoid the crowds. But if your guide has never been to Orlando before, you're probably going to have a disillusioning experience at Disney World. You'll probably spend a lot of time in long lines. It's the same way in the other worlds.

An initiate woke up in a dream and saw a maze of streets. Three children were coming down one of the streets toward her. "Do you know where our father is?" they asked.

The dreamer had been this route before. "Sure," she said and gave the three children directions. Looking at it with spiritual symbology, the children were Souls, and they were saying, "Do you know where the Mahanta, the Dream Master, is?"

*Looking at it with spiritual symbology, the children were Souls, and they were saying, "Do you know where the Mahanta, the Dream Master, is?"*

Two of them ran off immediately because that was all the direction they needed. Soon they were out of sight. But the third child seemed to be having difficulties; he was a little slower in walking. The dreamer felt that the child had karmic problems which made it difficult for him to progress on the spiritual path.

The dreamer guided the child through the streets. They kept up a pleasant conversation about one thing or another, until finally they came to a wall that had a window in it, decorated with lights and little teddy bears.

"Here's the window," the dreamer said to the little

boy. "I don't know how you're going to get through it."

"Oh, I know how," the boy said. "And I know what to do when I get through it. I get in the boat and row to the island, and there's my father."

When the dreamer awoke, she knew that no matter how inadequate she sometimes felt about her knowledge of ECK, she had something to give to others. She could act as a guide on the inner planes, working with the Dream Master to show people how to make the spiritual connection with the Mahanta.

This is one example of how an ECK initiate works with other Souls in the dream state. In this case, the little boy trying to find the island was a symbol of Soul looking for the Isle of Bliss, or Paradise.

*An ECK initiate works with other Souls in the dream state.*

## PRACTICE BRINGS SUCCESS

An Arahata told my wife and me about some of the ways he works with other initiates in an ECK Satsang class. He helps them learn about the Light and Sound of God. "Sometimes I'll ask them to use an imaginative technique," he said. "For instance, I'll say, 'See if you can visualize a waterfall.'"

Just like that I saw a huge, beautiful waterfall. My wife and I looked at each other and started to laugh—she had seen the waterfall too.

But the Arahata found that not everyone has success with the imaginative technique. Some people cannot even visualize something as simple as a waterfall.

To reassure those of you who have a hard time with visualization, it does become easier. Like anything else, if you keep doing it again and again, you're going to get better at it, because that's just how it is.

People who seem to be natural athletes, or have a natural talent for cooking, sewing, writing, or anything else, have paid their dues. You can believe that. Sometime in the past they made cakes that fell, sewed dresses with uneven hemlines, or wrote manuscripts that didn't sell or that required many painful rewrites before they sold.

It's difficult for the average person to realize the very hard work that lies behind someone else's success. It's easy to say, "Well, he's always been that way." It sounds as if the talent came out of nowhere. But this is not so. At some point in the past, that individual, as Soul, had to learn the hard way. He had to make mistakes. He had to practice over and over, until the talent became smooth, became second nature, began to flow with the individual as smoothly as the invisible river of life.

## AN APPLE FOR THE TEACHER

Sometimes people overlook the value of the spiritual exercises given at these talks because they are simple. I keep them simple for a reason: they are easy to remember and easy to do. Anything too complicated will either be forgotten by the time you get back to your room or will seem like too much work.

The exercise I'd like to give here is very simple: Just imagine yourself back in grade school—in parochial school if you like—bringing a gift of some kind to the teacher. If you're an ECKist, you can bring the gift to the Mahanta. Those of another faith can bring it to the teacher of that faith.

A certain dreamer decided to bring an apple to the Mahanta, the Dream Master. As she waited to give him this gift, she began to have doubts about her choice: *I should have brought a peach instead,* she thought. *That would have been a more perfect gift.*

She handed the apple to the Dream Master,

*A certain dreamer decided to bring an apple to the Mahanta, the Dream Master.*

thinking about the peach she should have brought. Suddenly she happened to glance down, and in his hand she saw a heart.

She realized then that the gift didn't matter— it wasn't important whether she brought an apple or a peach. What mattered was that she brought it with her heart.

*ECK Summer Festival, Orlando, Florida,*
*Saturday, June 10, 1989*

We are all part of the community of ECK.

# 10

# THE TEMPLE OF ECK

The setting for the Temple of ECK is suburban Minnesota, a land of lawn mowers and snow throwers.

In my neighborhood there seems to be a lot of competition with regard to lawn care. The people really get upset if their lawn is cut and yours isn't. You can usually measure the degree of friction between neighbors by how much higher or lower one's grass is compared to the other's. A difference of four inches signals a serious anger factor.

## SETTING STANDARDS

This year I've been trying to set the standard in my neighborhood. I decided to mow the lawn the weekend before we left for the seminar so my neighbors wouldn't have any cause for complaint, but I didn't get to it on Saturday. By that evening my next-door neighbor thought he was getting the weekend off.

Right before dark on Sunday night, I got the mower out and cut the grass, finishing the job just as it got too dark to see. And by then the mosquitoes

One can reach a certain peak spiritually, but it counts for nothing if you don't cut your lawn.

were driving me wild. But as soon as I got in the house, I heard the lawn mower start up next door.

This is part of the environment for the Temple of ECK. One can reach a certain peak spiritually, but it counts for nothing if you don't cut your lawn.

## BUSY SIGNAL

Another thing that has been pushing me to the very edge is my computer. I stretched my skills so that I could log into a computer information service. The main reason was to use a particular database that has an encyclopedia. I figured it would be helpful in my research as I write ECK materials.

But before you even get near the point where you can download from these computer information services, you have to learn practically everything that has happened in the computer field since the development of the first chip. One thing I learned was how little I actually knew about modems.

One night I sat in front of my computer, trying to call the local telephone number to log into the computer information service. "Busy signal. Try again later," the computer screen informed me. I tried over and over, checked everything out, and still couldn't get the connection.

Several tries into the night, I discovered that I didn't have the modem plugged into the telephone connection on the wall. The computer had been going through all the proper motions, but it couldn't get out of the house. Things like this keep you humble.

## A SPIRITUAL CENTER

The Temple of ECK is a spiritual temple. A search for land has been under way for the past decade, but always with the idea of finding the right location for a Seat of Power and a spiritual center. This is the first time we actively looked for land with the goal of building the Temple of ECK. Once we have built the Temple, we will make it the Seat of Power.

This is a subtle distinction, but it's there: build the Temple first, and then make it the Seat of Power. Our main emphasis now is on the spiritual element — the Temple of ECK.

## On a Dotted Line

*The Temple represents a very important milestone in the history of Eckankar.*

The Temple represents a very important milestone in the history of Eckankar. It stands on a dotted line that separates the microcosm from the macrocosm of the potential of the ECK teachings in the world today. Words like *microcosm* and *macrocosm* slip off the tongue very easily, but some of you are probably wondering, What exactly is he talking about?

When the teachings of Eckankar were first brought out in 1965, Paul Twitchell talked about the individuality of Soul. He meant Soul in Its full sense, but people often understood it in the small, or microcosmic, sense. It was a selfish interpretation of the works of ECK and of the ECK initiate's responsibilities and place in the world.

The misunderstanding went like this: I will gain spiritual freedom; I will get God-Realization; and I will become a law unto myself. While these precepts are not false, they were only a splinter of the entire teaching that Paul was trying to give out. It was a selfish, egotistical look at one's place in the cosmic order. The individual sought God-Realization and freedom. But he never took it a step further to say, What does God-Realization lead to?

## SERVING OTHERS

A few who proclaimed themselves God-Realized figured the next logical step was, I shall gather unto myself a small band of followers who will consider me their leader. This is not the purpose.

If one really has attained God-Realization, he touches many people in a natural way. If he doesn't have God-Realization, he generally never touches very many people in a significant, spiritual way at all.

So what we had in the past were some who thought only of themselves and their own spiritual good. On the microcosmic, small side of the dotted line, their attitude was: I seek consciousness for myself. In the macrocosmic worlds, it changes to: I seek consciousness so that I may serve life.

Yes, Soul is an individual; It retains Its individuality beyond all time, beyond all universes. But It retains Its individuality to be a Co-worker with God, to help others find their way to the Light and Sound of God. This is Soul's mission.

## WE ARE ALL SOUL

The old way of understanding the teachings led to introversion. People were closed. They didn't really want the teachings of ECK to go out to the world; they wanted to keep feeling that they were different.

But the fact is, we are not different from other people—we are all Soul. This was what people in the microcosmic order of ECK forgot, and so they put forth their own spirituality at the expense of others.

Some people use the idea of past lives in order to feel better about their low station in this life. "I was King or Queen So-and-So in the fifteenth century," they'll say, strutting regally with their noses in the air. It doesn't occur to them that we were all royalty at some point in the past.

So you see the point: In the past there was a very narrow interpretation of the teachings of ECK. What I am doing today is bringing the teachings to the whole world. This is the natural, spiritual order of things to come and to be.

## A HOME FOR ECKANKAR

If we wish to understand what is to be and what is right, we simply study the laws of nature. Nature shows how truth has manifested itself in the past. Some truth never became established in an outer form because that was not its purpose, and so it quickly disappeared.

But at other times, truth manifested outwardly in the form of mosques, temples, churches, synagogues, and prayer lodges. Putting a structure into the physical world of form insures a longer life.

The Temple of ECK provides a house for the teachings of ECK on the physical plane. It is a gathering place for outer and inner study. All who come to the outer temple, physically, may also come to the inner temple—in the dream state, in contemplation, and via Soul Travel—to study the holy works of ECK.

The Temple is a way station between the physical and the spiritual worlds, occupying its place along with the four other major Temples of Golden Wisdom on the physical plane.

## PROVING OURSELVES

It was a rugged challenge to get approval to build the Temple from the city council of Chanhassen, a suburb about ten miles west-southwest of Minneapolis—St. Paul.

*Nature shows how truth has manifested itself in the past.*

In 1985 we had tried to get zoning permits from the city council, but with the ECK Office still in California, we were too far away to pursue it. When the council did not accept our request for a zoning change, we decided to wait until we could move to Minnesota. Then we could establish ourselves and show that ECK initiates are responsible individuals.

We had proven that in California and had very good recommendations from the public-safety officers in Menlo Park. But despite all the support from people who knew us, we were moving into a new community. Minnesotans are cautious people — it's part of their Midwestern nature — and they wanted to see for themselves.

## CHALLENGES

Some of you knew the challenges we faced as we went through the voting process with the city council of Chanhassen. I'm grateful that you did not show up in Minnesota to camp out on the grounds and make a spiritual stand. There are better ways to do things. We would like to work harmoniously with the city of Chanhassen in the future and continue to build good relations with the residents.

The city council voted 5-0 to allow us to build the Temple. But this doesn't signal a wholehearted endorsement of Eckankar. Some of the council members were less than enthusiastic, yet they didn't want to go on record with an opposing voice vote. There are a few people in Chanhassen who are vocally against us, though we had much support from the majority of the community. A few people went out of their way to say, "We do not agree with those who are taking such a stand against you, and we just want you to know it."

In every era there is conflict of this nature. The vocal few make their voices heard loud enough to try to convince others that they are the majority. But they were not the majority; the record shows that the vote was unanimous in our favor. The feelings were not quite so unanimous, of course, so it will take time for a healing to come about.

## HELP FROM OUR FRIENDS

It would have been impossible for Eckankar to even consider building the Temple of ECK in Chanhassen were it not for the help of many of our friends and associates in the community. Christians and Jews alike helped bring our dream of the Temple of ECK to this point.

The cooperation of people of different religions, helping to bring about the Temple of ECK as a physical manifestation, is significant. This is the purpose of the ECK teachings: to uplift all the religions of the world.

You cannot uplift something by trying to destroy it or saying, "We are better than you, our teachings are more pure." Every religion teaches that, otherwise it would have nothing to offer its people. Each group feels it has the highest spiritual teachings.

As our associates from other faiths worked with us on this project, some of them began to notice how the ECK operates. For example, during one meeting in which decisions were being made about certain conditions that had come up, the lights in the room suddenly flared brighter.

"Is that the ECK?" they asked.

"Yes," an ECK initiate said. "That's an example of the Holy Spirit. I think we should be listening to what It's saying." So they began to listen to the signs

*As our associates from other faiths worked with us on this project, some of them began to notice how the ECK operates.*

or manifestations of the Holy Spirit as It guided them in making the decisions to bring about the first stage of the approvals. The hand of the Holy Spirit has been in there every step of the way.

## NATURAL LAWS AND CYCLES

To understand ourselves and our place in the world, we might pay more attention to the natural laws, to the life cycles of animals and plants. In the case of a young plant, you water it, but not too much; you fertilize it, but not too much. And if you do everything correctly—give it the proper temperature, the proper amount of sunlight—the plant will grow and bloom. On the other hand, if you neglect the steps required for growth, the plant suffers. Then you have to start over again and take extra time to bring the plant back to health and beauty.

When the cycle of the healthy young plant reaches the stage where it blossoms, you then have to put it into a larger pot. This is the only way it can thrive and grow some more.

*The ECK teachings came to the point where we had to find a larger pot.*

The ECK teachings came to the point where we had to find a larger pot. This is absolutely essential in order to reach more people with the teachings of the Light and Sound of God.

Gardeners have a saying: A plant will always grow enough to fill the pot it's in. So even if sometimes it seems as though the pot is too big, I don't worry about it. The ECK will fill it; the plant will grow.

## THE TEMPLE IS NEWS

We've had an interesting response to the publicity in the Minneapolis–St. Paul area over our attempts to build the Temple of ECK. There was a great controversy, and for a while the newspapers and TV stations wanted interviews. We then had to face a decision: Did we want to refuse to give interviews? Or should we present our side of the story, even though some of the Christian public had been hostile to us? Finally we decided that it would be best to go ahead and talk to them.

For the most part, the news media treated us with fairness, but there were a few exceptions. Occasionally they indulged in yellow journalism and compared ECK with other groups to slant the facts. There was no basis for making the comparisons, but they did it anyway. Sometimes we let it go, but other times we called the editor of the newspaper or TV station and had it corrected.

An interesting change took place after we won the right to build the Temple of ECK. Up to that point the controversy was news, so we regularly made the headlines: "Eckankar plans to build temple in Chanhassen!" But when we got the city-council vote, the Minneapolis newspaper carried only a very short announcement back on page 5: "Eckankar wins 5-0 approval to build temple in Chanhassen." Our win didn't merit much fervor; it wasn't news.

*An interesting change took place after we won the right to build the Temple of ECK.*

## GROWTH AND PROSPERITY

We moved to Minnesota in 1986, and the Minnesota Twins won the World Series the following year. We were all very happy—it was like a hello to us. It put nationwide attention on Minneapolis. I feel it happened because the presence of the ECK moved in.

The 1992 Super Bowl will be held in Minneapolis. When our governor announced his intention to meet with the football commissioners to keep Minneapolis in the bidding, the local sportscasters made light of his efforts. "Our governor should stay home," one proclaimed on the nightly news. "He hasn't a chance of winning the Super Bowl for Minneapolis." They felt that the only chance the governor would ever have was if he built a dome over the city, to protect attendees from the harsh weather. Without a climate-controlled environment, they were sure people wouldn't come.

The governor went anyway and came home with the prize—the Super Bowl of 1992. Again, an event that will put a lot of attention on Minneapolis–St. Paul. It will also result in building better hotel facilities and other amenities, all of which will remain long after the Super Bowl is over.

The influence of the ECK is also seen in another way. A few days from now, Minneapolis will host ground-breaking ceremonies for one of the largest shopping malls in the world.

With such a huge, enclosed shopping area, the city hopes to draw a lot more tourists, which means even more hotel facilities. By the time we're ready to hold seminars in Minneapolis, there will be more for you to enjoy, even during the winter. The ECK is arranging for all this even before the need arises. Once again, we are seeing the hand of the Holy Spirit at work in the community which will house the Temple of ECK.

*We are seeing the hand of the Holy Spirit at work in the community which will house the Temple of ECK.*

## WEDDING DRESS DREAM

A Higher Initiate in Minneapolis was starting an ECK dream class. She got a call from an elderly woman who had learned about Eckankar through the publicity over our efforts to build in Chanhassen. What intrigued her the most were the terms *Soul Travel* and *dream study*.

In the past the woman had had several out-of-

body experiences, but she didn't know what they
were all about. She hadn't realized that there was
a name for them. She came from an orthodox background. Though she felt that her dreams had much
to teach her, she didn't know how to go about studying them. She was interested in the *ECK Dream
Discourses* which come with ECK membership.

The elderly woman went on to tell the Higher
Initiate about a dream she'd had just as she decided
to look into the ECK study program. In the dream
she was wearing a wedding dress. "I saw it as the
end of something old and the beginning of something
new," she said.

I thought that was an interesting way to put it.
Usually we think of a wedding in terms of the future,
without realizing that it also means the end of an
old way of life, something we have outgrown.

## TUNNEL, LIGHT, AND LOVE

The woman was a hospice volunteer who worked
with AIDS patients. She had studied under Elisabeth
Kübler-Ross and had learned that many AIDS patients have the inner experience of a tunnel, the
Light, and love.

In ECK we want to add the Sound to this experience. The Light and Sound is the Voice of God. The
Light takes us into the lower heavens, and the Sound
lifts Soul beyond that, into the higher planes of pure
Spirit. We would like to go as far as we can.

We all know that AIDS has come to touch those
outside the gay community. When the first cases
turned up, the condition was associated primarily
with gay people. Certain preachers showed a lot of
insensitivity, calling it God's curse upon these people,
and so on.

*The Light takes
us into the
lower heavens,
and the Sound
lifts Soul
beyond that,
into the higher
planes of pure
Spirit.*

Those particular preachers certainly were not speaking for all Christians, since so many Christians do have compassion and understanding. But regardless, you don't lord it over someone in their time of illness or hardship. What's the point? Even if you believe it's God's punishment, then let God take care of it. God doesn't need his imperfect little human beings giving out their imperfect, distorted judgments that supposedly are God's.

*Whereas many AIDS patients have experiences with the tunnel, the Light, and love, I would say that few moralists ever do.*

Yet, this is how those on the fringes of Christianity so often react. They profess to speak for God, and they can't; they don't have love and they don't have compassion. And you can always recognize them— "by their deeds shall ye know them."

It's sad, and yet there is an element here that I find interesting: The people who contract AIDS, who are labeled morally degenerate by these fringe Christians, are actually led to higher spiritual experiences and understandings than their critics. Whereas many AIDS patients have experiences with the tunnel, the Light, and love, I would say that few moralists ever do.

## WHY BUILD AN ECK TEMPLE?

A group of ECKists in Minnesota were discussing why there should be a Temple of ECK. Many of them were opposed to it, fearing that it would lead to more regimentation.

They were thinking in the small, narrow sense of "I have truth, and that's enough." They didn't consider what it might take to carry this truth out into the world. It didn't occur to them that by giving up their small ideas of the past and thus becoming greater in consciousness themselves, they could help in the greater mission of ECK.

So they were having this discussion, and it was going against the Temple of ECK. Finally a person who had remained quiet through the meeting asked, "May I speak?"

The group turned their attention to him. "Though I have just become a member of Eckankar," he said, "I've been studying the teachings for many years. The reason I decided to join was that I heard about the plans to build the Temple. I figured Eckankar was finally getting its act together."

This new student of ECK understood that the laws of nature require that certain steps be taken to bring truth into this world. The Temple provides another vessel for truth. As I said before, the Temple of ECK is the fifth main Temple of Golden Wisdom on the physical plane, a place where initiates and acolytes can gather for inner and outer Satsang classes.

*The laws of nature require that certain steps be taken to bring truth into this world.*

The Temple of ECK has theater-style seating, not pews—which, incidentally, was very difficult for our architect to comprehend. Nor do we have an organ. We'll have a piano, and sometimes guest musicians playing flute, harp, guitar, or other instruments, but the music will always be uplifting. I have nothing against organs except that the music is often dreary for a spiritual setting. During the ECK Worship Services, we may even show videos at times, to give attendees an understanding of what it means to be part of the cosmic system of ECK.

## GREATER LAWS

We are not a law unto ourselves, except spiritually. Out here we operate under the laws of the physical universe, and that includes the laws of the city and state. If you doubt this, then drive through downtown at sixty miles per hour and try to explain it to the traffic officer who pulls you over.

It is simplistic to say we are a law unto ourselves and think it means: I will act irresponsibly in my community. This is not so. We, as ECKists, are required spiritually to act with the greatest degree of responsibility, both to ourselves and to others. This is what it means to be part of the community of ECK and part of the cosmic system of life. It all fits together.

*We are an atom in the Ocean of Love and Mercy, but we are not the only atom.*

We are an atom in the Ocean of Love and Mercy, but we are not the only atom. If we were, there would be no Ocean. We are important only because all the other Souls are important. We are equally important before God, the Sugmad. Because if one Soul isn't, then none of them are. But if one is, then all are.

## BANANAS

I read an article in the *Washington Post* by Sandy Rovner. It told the story of an old man from Burma whose lovely young daughter married a handsome student.

Though the couple were very happy, the old man was worried about his daughter's future with such an impractical husband. He felt that his son-in-law had no sense of how to make his living in this world.

The young man was an alchemist. He was certain that if he studied long and hard enough, he would find the secret of turning base material into gold. The old man knew better, and finally he thought of a way to address the problem.

One day he invited his son-in-law to his home. As soon as his guest arrived, the old man made a show of carefully locking the doors and closing all the windows. Then he said, "I understand you are an alchemist."

"Yes, I am," his son-in-law said.

"I am too," the old man said. "And I have found the secret."

"You did?" The young man was astonished.

"Yes, and I'll teach it to you," the old man offered. In a confidential tone he went on to reveal the secret: "On the bottom of the banana leaf is a fine, silvery powder. But in order to get this powder, you must first have banana leaves. You have to scrape off the powder until you get five pounds. It takes a long time to gather even an ounce, yet you must have five pounds before you can turn base material into gold."

The young man couldn't wait to get started. He went off to plant banana trees, and as they grew, he very carefully scraped off the silver dust from the bottom of the leaves.

Many years later, the young man and his wife went to visit his father-in-law. "I've got five pounds of the silver dust," he announced.

"Very good," the old man said. "But what did you do with the bananas?"

"I sold them so that we could live," his daughter said.

"Do you have any savings?" he asked.

"Oh, yes," she said, putting a cloth bag on the table. "I sold the bananas all these years, used the money wisely, and managed to acquire this purseful of gold."

The old man went outside and got a handful of dirt. Placing it on the table beside the purse, he said, "See? You've turned base elements into gold."

So often in our spiritual unfoldment we are like the young alchemist. We want to make the big leap, but we want to take a shortcut. We will work so hard at the shortcut that unless there is someone with

*We want to make the big leap, but we want to take a shortcut.*

common sense—like the Dream Master—to help us back into balance, we waste our time. We live a life of hardship and make life unbearable for our loved ones we are to provide for. But through experience we eventually learn that life is the sweat and toil of raising bananas.

## SPIRITUAL GOLD

This is what brought the gold. The silver powder on the bottom of the leaves had nothing to do with it, except to act as inspiration. And the silver dust was the inspiration of a very wise old man. He's like the Dream Master.

This also is what the Temple of ECK and the teachings of Eckankar are to accomplish: to turn base elements into spiritual gold.

If you keep your spiritual senses open, you will see the ways of ECK working through other people, trying to teach you by experience about the wisdom of life. And as you go home, I want you to know that I am always with you.

May the blessings be.

*If you keep your spiritual senses open, you will see the ways of ECK working through other people.*

*ECK Summer Festival, Orlando, Florida, Sunday, June 11, 1989*

Dreams are working continuously in our lives, not only when we are asleep but also when we are awake. The universal nature of dreams encompasses the universal being, Soul.

# 11

# The Universal Nature of Dreams, Part 1

*T*he universal nature of dreams transcends the various cultures. Symbols may vary from place to place, but these are minute details. To deal with dreams from the level of symbols is to treat them in a light, superficial way.

By *the universal nature of dreams,* I mean that dreams are working continuously in our lives. They are working not only when we are asleep but also when we are awake. The universal nature of dreams encompasses the universal being, Soul.

*Dreams are working continuously in our lives.*

## Everything Needs Love

For a while I kept an eye on a nest that a pair of robins had built in a small tree in our yard. Robins are very neat in building their nests. This one, nice and round, was fixed firmly in the branches so that it wouldn't fall out, even in a bad storm.

On the other hand, there is the common house sparrow, who will make a nest wherever it feels like. When a screen fell out of an air conditioning vent at the side of our house, we found a ragged nest with two house sparrows. They were just as happy in the air conditioning vent as the robins were in the little tree.

One evening I was out working in the yard. I had just finished mowing the grass and was setting up the hoses to water my geraniums, a gay mixture of white, pink, and red. They're set along the driveway to greet me when I come home. Some of my neighbors have commented on how nice they look.

One neighbor, being pulled down the sidewalk by his huge dog, stopped to tell me how pretty the geraniums were. "Plants need love just like animals," I said. "Just like your dog."

I think I caught him off guard. He must have just gotten home from work. Tired and hungry, he still had to take the dog out for its duty walk before he could relax and have dinner. It was probably the last thing he felt like doing right then.

But after I made that comment, he looked at his dog as if to say, "Excuse me for being so rude. I understand why you must have your walk."

## WAKING-LIFE LESSONS

This man was an example of the universal dreamer. In the course of his everyday life, through his own ears, he got a lesson on how to treat his pet better.

I didn't say it to preach to him. Actually, it didn't even occur to me until after I spoke that he might have been a little upset about having to take the dog for a walk. But it was part of his waking dream to meet with a neighbor who would awaken him to be more conscious of what he was doing in his daily chores.

*The reason we learn so much at ECK seminars is that they provide a change of view.*

Many times we don't like our chores and duties. We have done them so often that they've become a drudgery and lost their meaning. We have gone to sleep spiritually. The reason we learn so much at ECK seminars is that they provide a change of view.

We are doing something new. And because we have left our routines at home, we are more open to the voice of ECK.

Our daily waking life is part of the universal nature of dreams. But sometimes we are led out of the routine. It was very important for the man to walk his dog, and it was very important for me to care for my geraniums at that time.

*Our daily waking life is part of the universal nature of dreams.*

## A Fallen Robin

My neighbor and his dog continued on their walk. As I turned back to the geraniums, I kept hearing a peeping sound, like a little bird in distress, followed by the song of a full-grown robin. What was all the commotion about?

I followed the sound to the tree, and that's when I found the nest. In it were two young robins. The parent robins were off gathering worms to feed into those young beaks.

At this point I saw a third robin. It had fallen out of the nest and was lying at the base of the tree. The nest had become almost too small for three robins. This one must have carelessly walked to the edge of the nest and slipped off.

The parents probably had mixed feelings when they saw their little one on the ground at the base of the tree. They were very distressed, yet their instincts drove them to feed only the babies in the nest.

## Karmic Choice

I watched for a while to see if the parents would return and carry food to the young robin that had fallen out of the tree. I also thought about the large cat that prowled the neighborhood, looking for birds. Would he come tonight? What if he was hungry? Now I was really worried about the young robin.

The parents did not return to feed the fallen baby bird. It appeared they were going to let it starve. So now I was faced with a dilemma, just like the crew of the spaceship *Enterprise* on the "Star Trek" TV series. Although their mission was to go where no one had ever gone before, they were not supposed to interfere in the karma of anyone they met on the planets they visited.

So I'm standing by the geraniums, wondering whether to interfere in this little family's karma. If I pick up the bird and place it back in the nest, will the parents smell the human touch and abandon all three of the young robins? We make our own world, of course, and the choice was mine.

*We make our own world.*

I waited a little longer. Now and then the baby robin on the ground would make a small peeping sound. It would look up at the nest, not knowing how to get back there, too young to fly. It was afraid that it would never see home again.

But every so often it would try to tell itself, "I'm a big bird; I'm not afraid of anything." Then it would make the sound of a full-grown robin. And so I had heard the peep-peep of a frightened baby bird and the confident song of a grown robin. The little bird was torn back and forth.

Finally I decided that I had to do something. I went to the garage and looked around for something to pick the robin up with. Fortunately, the nest in that small tree was just a little higher than my head, so I would have no problem placing the little robin back in its home.

I emerged from the garage carrying a small garden trowel and a broken-off broomstick. Approaching the tree, I could tell that the little bird did not like me at all. It gave me the sourest of looks, as if to say,

"You touch me and I'll . . ." *You'll what, little bird?* I inquired silently.

I scooped it onto the center of the trowel and held the broomstick in front, so the bird couldn't fall off. With both hands occupied, I had to be very careful that the trowel didn't tip over as I lifted it up to the nest. The baby robin might not be able to withstand another fall.

Just as I got the trowel level with the nest, one of the parents returned. I couldn't tell if it was the mother or the father. My wife tried to explain that the male robin has a reddish-orange breast while the female's is a less flashy orange. But since the mother and father weren't there at the same time, I had no way to compare them.

The parent bird perched on a branch right by my face and started making a big fuss. I was pretty sure it was saying, "Don't touch my baby! Please don't hurt my baby!" In the meantime, I'm trying to get the bird into the nest, but it's resisting. The other two siblings have spread their feathers out, and there's not enough room.

I'm nudging the young bird off the trowel with the stick, and it's hanging half out of the nest. "This is your only chance," I said. "If you want to grow up, get in." That little bird gave me the dirtiest look. It was probably thinking, *A steel trowel and an ordinary stick are my only chance?*

Finally I got the robin in the nest. The siblings grudgingly made room for it, but they were not too happy to see who'd come back. This was no long-lost brother coming home to a joyful reunion.

The mother or the father—I could never tell—stayed on the branch, scolding, nervous, hopping around, very excited. I took the hint and went away, but I asked my wife to help me keep an eye out. I wanted to make sure that the little bird stayed put.

## LITTLE THANKS FOR THE HELP

The next morning I checked again, and all three young robins were in the nest. But then I noticed something very interesting. Two of the birds looked so innocent and trusting, their little beaks opened toward the sky, waiting for Mom or Dad to come flying home with another worm. But the third bird—and I knew who it was right away—had his mouth shut and his eyes open. And he gave me the same sour look that he had the day before. "You're not the first one," I said. "I've helped others and gotten just as much thanks."

The young robins stayed in the nest for another nine days. But every time I went to look in on them, I could always tell which one had been out of the nest too soon. The worldly-wise little robin kept his mouth closed, but he always had his eyes wide open. I don't know if I did the world a favor or not.

I've always thought of robins as proud, feisty little George Washingtons. They fit my image of him in his greatcoat, standing straight and tall with his chest puffed out. And you just don't pick up George Washington with a metal trowel and a wooden stick.

## GREATER DESTINY

One morning shortly after that my wife said, "There are a lot of robins out in the backyard. Something seems to be the matter." Looking out the window, I saw five or six robins roaming the lawn. Now that the three young birds had moved out of the tree in the front yard, the parents had invited a relative to come over and help initiate them into their greater new life.

I could imagine the instructions the grown-up robins gave as they showed the young ones around the yard: "Look what a big world you have come to. Now that you can fly, you no longer have to stay on the ground or worry about falling out of nests. Of course, there are other worries now, like cats. So watch where you pick the worms. Don't get too near the bushes."

In a way, this also is part of the universal nature of dreams. The little birds in the nest are like people before they find the Light and Sound of God. They're in the little nest and feel they are safe and secure. Somebody is always taking care of them. Life is just perfect. Ignorance is bliss. But gradually life becomes less and less perfect as these little creatures grow bigger and the nest starts to get crowded.

There are stirrings within the little bird that say its destiny is greater than this little nest, which is growing smaller every day. After all, how long can you eat somebody else's worms? You want to spread your wings and see if there's something else out in the world besides worms. You might eventually settle for that, but first you want to see for yourself.

These little birds are like Soul before It finds truth. The natural order of life is growth and spiritual unfoldment. Whether you like it or not, believe it or not, or want to accept it or not, life says you are going to grow spiritually, until someday you outgrow your present state of consciousness.

*The little birds in the nest are like people before they find the Light and Sound of God.*

## Early Spiritual Experiences

It's a very fearful time when an individual comes to the point of outgrowing his state of consciousness, especially if he falls out of the nest before he is ready. In other words, some people have an experience in the dream worlds or with the Light and Sound before they are spiritually mature. They will most likely misread the help of the Inner Master who says, "It's too soon for you. You're not ready to be in the bigger world yet, because to survive out there, you have to fly. You are spiritually and physically unable to fly; therefore, I'm going to put you back in the nest."

But Soul never forgets that experience. Whether it's a vivid dream, Soul Travel, or an experience with the Light or Sound of God, it sticks in the individual's mind. Sometime later, all of a sudden he's big enough to fly; he leaves the nest. Now he has a whole new world to explore and an entire summer in which to learn about his new life. When winter comes, he learns to fly south, to go with the seasons. He has his whole life to learn about living.

Spiritually, this has happened to you, the ECK initiate. You were once a young robin who fell out of the nest before your time. You had an experience that showed you there is more to life than you knew up to that moment—something greater than the nest of the human consciousness. The Inner Master, or one of the ECK Masters, helped you back into your state of consciousness until you were strong enough spiritually to venture forth into these new worlds yourself. And at the moment you were able to fly freely, to find the nourishment that you needed spiritually, you entered a whole new world.

*Now that you are able to see the connection between your inner and outer lives, you would never be happy returning to the nest.*

Many of you have gone through the beginning steps of the inner experiences and are having outer experiences through waking dreams or the Golden-tongued Wisdom. Now that you are able to see the connection between your inner and outer lives, you would never be happy returning to the nest.

Of course, there are people who try. But that's like a young bird trying to get back into the eggshell.

## DREAMS THAT COME TOO SOON

An initiate once had an experience in which I told her to find ECK and Eckankar. It happened in 1966, less than a year after Paul Twitchell brought the teachings of Eckankar to the public. She was eleven years old at the time, fourteen years away from an understanding of what her dream meant.

The initiate had a very difficult childhood. Her brother died when she was just eleven and, as can be expected, she was left feeling very sad.

It had already been discovered that she had tuberculosis, and while still grieving for her brother, she had to undergo a lung operation. During her monthlong recuperation, she began to have a series of dreams. A man she had never seen before told her: "Find ECK. Find Eckankar."

When she got out of the hospital, she searched through every dictionary and encyclopedia she could get her hands on, but nowhere did she find the words *ECK* and *Eckankar*. *What,* she wondered, *were those strange dreams all about?*

A year later, her grandparents were in a serious automobile accident. About one o'clock one morning she dreamed that a man wearing a blue shirt and blue slacks came to her grandmother and escorted her to the other side. She had no idea who the man in blue was.

In ECK we know that blue is traditionally the color worn by the spiritual leader of Eckankar. The Mahanta, the Living ECK Master of the time usually appears in blue both inwardly and outwardly.

She awoke and went downstairs to tell her father about the dream. "A man in blue took Grandmother across to the other side," she said. Her family lived in a remote area with no telephone, so they were unable

*A man she had never seen before told her: "Find ECK. Find Eckankar."*

She had glimpsed the future through the ECK-Vidya, but, like a little bird fallen from the nest, she wasn't ready to handle it.

to check it out right then. But the next day an aunt drove over to break the news: the grandmother had died—at one o'clock the previous morning.

Foreseeing this event put a terrible strain on the young girl. She had glimpsed the future through the ECK-Vidya, but, like a little bird fallen from the nest, she wasn't ready to handle it. Nor could she deal with the other experiences that occurred around the same time, such as seeing the ghost of an American Indian walk through the house.

She knew that her father kept his bourbon and other hard liquor on the top shelf of a cabinet. One day, in an effort to blot out the memory of her inner experiences, she took her first drink. She found that the more she drank, the less she remembered. For the next fourteen years she lived pretty much in a drunken stupor, trying to forget what she had seen.

The time came when she knew she had to give up alcohol, and soon after that, she met a man. She thought he had the happiest face she had ever seen. They went out on a few dates, and after they became better acquainted, he began to tell her about ECK and Eckankar.

The first time he said the word *Eckankar*, she almost ended the relationship. She was immediately reminded of the dream of her grandmother's death and all the other experiences that had frightened her so much. But she had matured since then, and she also saw that this man was peaceful and happy. Soon after that they were married, and to this day they are happily together.

This was an instance where the dream came to the baby robin too soon. But still, the message was being presented: There is a bigger, brighter world waiting for you. When the time is right, you will be ready to enter into this world and enjoy a fuller life than you can ever imagine.

## THE MOTORCYCLE MAN

Another ECKist told me about her experiences with "the motorcycle man." She was only three or four years of age when they began.

Every night, just before she went to sleep, she would hear a motorcycle coming down the street. The driver would rev the motor as he brought it in through the front door and down to the basement. She could hear the motor humming very quietly as the driver came up the stairs. But as soon as he walked into her room, she would quickly close her eyes.

She was always afraid when the man on the motorcycle came while she was physically awake. But when she shut her eyes, the fear would dissolve. She could then see things as Soul. And when the man said, "Want to go for a ride on the motorcycle?" she would immediately say, "Sure!"

*"You were only dreaming," they would say each time. But she knew it was more than a dream.*

Together they would walk down to the basement, ride out of the house on the motorcycle, and go on all kinds of adventures. The next morning she would wake up and run to tell her parents, "The motorcycle man gave me a ride again last night!" "You were only dreaming," they would say each time. But she knew it was more than a dream. The experiences with this kindly man, who was an ECK Master, went on for a couple of years.

## LIGHT AND SOUND

When she was twelve or thirteen, she had another type of experience. It gave her the feeling of vibration. This was the ECK, the Holy Spirit—the

Sound Itself. She also began to see the Light. It came down the hall while she was in her bedroom at night. The Light always frightened her, so she would shut her eyes and eliminate the scene from her mind.

She was now having experiences with the two aspects of the Holy Spirit, the Light and Sound of God. They manifest in many different ways, and she was experiencing them in her own way. Although they were very real, no one could explain them to her.

She was unable to sleep because of the Light coming down the hallway. When she told her parents about it, they decided to take her to a doctor. He gave her sleeping pills so that she could get her rest, and eventually the Light went away.

*Finally she began to pray, "Dear God, please come and stay by me. I need your love."*

This was the Inner Master coming in his Light body, which also is a manifestation of the Light of God. It's made out of the same spiritual fabric, you might say, as the cloth of God.

At the age of sixteen, the girl had a serious allergic reaction to a prescription medication. Too ill to get out of bed, she called out to her father. But it was late and he didn't hear her. Finally she began to pray, "Dear God, please come and stay by me. I need your love."

Once again, she saw this Light coming down the hall, but this time she wasn't afraid. The Light filled her room, and then It filled her heart with the most joyful love she had ever known.

Suddenly she felt herself being pulled out of the human shell. She found herself in the Soul body, in a world of beautiful Light and the sound of orchestral music more uplifting than she could have imagined. With the experience came healing, and when she awoke in bed, her fever was gone.

## LOOKING FOR HAPPINESS

Long after the experience was over, she often wondered how she could find that joy and happiness again. As she got older, she became interested in psychic phenomena, and once again she began to have inner experiences.

She told her mother about some of them, and also about the Light and Sound and the feelings of love she had experienced when she was sixteen. This time her mother did not suggest that she go to the doctor for sleeping pills. Instead, she handed her a copy of *The Tiger's Fang* by Paul Twitchell, saying, "I think you'll find your answers here." Her mother also told her about *ECKANKAR—The Key to Secret Worlds.* "That book will explain where you go during your inner experiences," she said.

The ECKist has since come to realize that the Light, the Sound, and the love are one and the same. They all go together.

*The Light, the Sound, and the love are one and the same. They all go together.*

## YOU ARE BIGGER THAN A BAD DREAM

My own inner worlds are usually enjoyable and sometimes challenging, but some of the experiences are very difficult to convey to others. There is a certain element that I can share with you in my talks or writings, and I do.

Sometimes situations come up that call for me to use every bit of knowledge that I have gained in the past in order to get out of them. So all I can say to those who write to me about their bad dreams is: Someday, as you get stronger, you will understand that you are bigger than the bad dream.

I am fortunate to be able to move about in this outer world and enjoy my work. Yet there have been times when I was so tired that I didn't feel I could do another thing. Then I would wonder, *If this is joy, then what's pain?* But sleep is a great rejuvenator, and it's also a joyful time to explore new worlds.

## VISITING INNER WORLDS

Sometimes I go back to worlds that I haven't visited since I was very young. Like an alumnus returning to his old school, I'll ask someone who lives there now to show me around.

I'll often walk through the corridors of places I visited years ago in my inner travels. At that time, of course, I called them dreams. But until I revisited many years later, I forgot that I'd ever had the dreams. Now I look around and remember coming there when I was twelve, fifteen, or twenty.

The people who live there now will point out the changes that have happened since I last visited. They'll show me the new construction and, in some cases, the renovations that were made to modernize older buildings. Sometimes I'll find that walls have been knocked down to make the rooms bigger. Whatever the changes, they always signify an upgrading of the structures.

I too have to go into the other worlds to catch up on the latest developments. The heavens are always changing—very much so. These travels into the inner worlds are visits to heaven; your dreams are visits to heaven.

## DREAMS ARE MEMORIES

Dreams are not merely symbolic messages from the subconscious, though many people accept them only in that way. Dreams may have symbolic messages, but only at the most superficial level. All the books listing thousands of dream symbols make much ado about nothing. Symbols are but the surface of the experience.

The dream world is actually an imperfectly remembered Soul Travel experience. When the memory is not very vivid, we call it a dream.

This is why I have linked Soul Travel and dream travel so closely together. Basically they are the same thing. They are not dreams, and they are not really Soul Travel. They are your experiences of life in greater worlds. And this is actually the best definition of Soul Travel: your experiences of life in the spiritual dimensions, in the greater worlds of God.

Unless you have the experience yourself, you can't really understand what it is all about. But these inner experiences are as important in gaining wisdom, knowledge, and understanding as any experience here on earth.

*The dream world is actually an imperfectly remembered Soul Travel experience.*

## THE UNIVERSAL NATURE OF DREAMS

This is why we speak of the universal nature of dreams. They affect both our inner and our outer lives. And they are not just dreams. They are consciousness. They are you as a conscious being having experiences.

This is why the Mahanta, the Living ECK Master of any age tries to find ways to help people who are on the borderline of orthodox thought and seeking the real truth. He tries to help them explore the inner worlds so that they can gain more wisdom and freedom. This is part of spiritual liberation. It is part of the package of God Consciousness—to be fully, universally aware of your own worlds at all hours of the day and night.

Along the way you have experiences that give you an understanding of the apparent mysteries that occur in everyday living. What is death? Why are some children so smart when they're only four or five years old? Why are some adults so ignorant at fifty and sixty years of age? These "mysteries" are revealed through an understanding of reincarnation and karma: How much experience has that Soul gained, or not gained, in previous lifetimes?

## GETTING TO KNOW YOURSELF

As you advance in your study of dreams and in your understanding of life, you gain a better knowledge of who and what you, yourself, are. In the process, you also gain a greater understanding of other people—who they are and why they act as they do.

A person with little or no spiritual awareness will not consider these things very important. "What's so great about that?" he'll say. "I've got a new car, a new home, and I'm at the head of this or that board of directors. This is what life's all about." But like the symbols in dreams, this is only a part of what life is all about.

*Imagine that you are having a conversation with me. Say, "Show me what I can do to help at the Temple of ECK."*

## TEMPLE OF ECK EXERCISE

I would like to give you a spiritual exercise that ties in with the Temple of ECK. As most of you know, the Temple is to be built in a suburb of Minneapolis, Minnesota.

Just before you go to sleep at night, close your eyes and chant HU several times. Imagine that you are having a conversation with me. Say, "Show me what I can do to help at the Temple of ECK." Then tell me what you are very good at doing or what you would like to do, and I'll put you to work.

As you do this exercise, imagine yourself typing a letter, cleaning the floor, washing windows,

building a door frame, painting a wall—or whatever else you think you do well. Even if it's something you don't think you are very good at but would
like to do, try that.

Always remember that you are working in the
Temple of ECK. The Temple of ECK is your own state
of consciousness. And if you ask me to put you to
work, I certainly will.

*The Temple of
ECK is your
own state of
consciousness.*

*ECK European Seminar, The Hague, Netherlands,
Saturday, July 29, 1989*

Dream. Dream your way home. Dream your way back to God. Use your creative imagination, because that's the only way you can return to the source of all life.

# 12

# THE UNIVERSAL NATURE OF DREAMS, PART 2

*M*any people feel that the spiritual leader of Eckankar can do as he pleases, but this is not the case. I work within very tight schedules. They come from both the inner and the outer. Everything has to go according to a certain schedule.

When instructions come through that Eckankar is to take a certain direction, sometimes it's as difficult for me to see the reason for it as it is for some of you. For instance, why call it the New-Age Religion? I had the same feelings that many of you did about the term *religion,* and so I had to reexamine the issue.

## ALL RELIGIONS COME FROM ECK

ECK is a spiritual teaching and a spiritual path, but the world recognizes religions. Yet there is an important distinction between the orthodox religions of old and the religion of ECK.

Some of you equate *spiritual* with "good" and *religion* with "bad." Keep in mind that all religions come from ECK; therefore, all religions have a purpose in the education of Soul. If this is their function

*Keep in mind that all religions come from ECK; therefore, all religions have a purpose in the education of Soul.*

as designated by the Sugmad and carried down through the Word of God, then it must be carried out by the Mahanta, the Living ECK Master. It's not a case of right or wrong. That's how it's coming down. That's how it's to be carried out, that's how it is.

Sometimes I too have to study a spiritual issue to see where I stand on it. It is not always easy to be completely "for" certain things. It takes me a while to get into it because I have to see why a thing is important.

## WHY A TEMPLE OF ECK?

When I examined the issue of a Temple of ECK, I realized that we have a long tradition of ECK Temples of Golden Wisdom. What's so unusual about another ECK Temple, especially one that is more accessible to people? The answer, of course, was That's how it is to be.

Why apologize for things that need no apology? At some point we just have to say, "That's how it is, and now we will see how to work with it."

## FORM AND SYSTEM

*It isn't the form of the Temple that's important, but the consciousness that fills it.*

It isn't the form of the Temple that's important, but the consciousness that fills it. It's the creative imagination of the people working within that structure as they find their experiences in life and serve God. This is what's important.

Any temporal forms, including religions and temples, are of the lower worlds and will pass. These forms may be around for a long time, but in the eyes of Soul, they are as nothing. They serve only as instruments and tools for the education of Soul. The forms are needed only as a way for people to learn.

Everything in the lower worlds responds to form

and system. Even people who want to be outside a form and system fit within one. The problem is not in the form or system but in their lack of understanding. The spiritual form is always there, but many are not aware of it.

## WHY DREAM?

We are working with the universal nature of dreams. In my talk last night, I was trying to get across a certain point: Why is it important for people to dream? Why should they care? Why should anyone in the audience care about dreams?"

Why are dreams important? It always comes back to Soul, the Eternal Dreamer. We form our existence through the creative imagination. This is the Sugmad's gift to Soul, to us.

And how does this creative imagination work down here in everyday living? It starts with a desire for something we would like to achieve. "I'm tired of living in apartments," we say, and this leads to the dream of building a home of our own.

## BUILDING SOUL'S HOME

This can be a spiritual desire. As the Eternal Dreamer, as immortal Soul, we are practicing how to create a better world for ourself, our family, and as many others as we can within our circle of influence. Yet we must always allow the people around us their own freedom, so that our dream does not intrude upon theirs.

The most successful people in the world dream, but they know it takes more than dreaming to reach a goal. You can't just dream about owning a home, you have to make plans; and plans fit into a form and system.

*We form our existence through the creative imagination. This is the Sugmad's gift to Soul, to us.*

You start to work out the details. How will you finance your home? You picture your home as it will be — a neat lawn, a pretty flower garden, trees, and birds. On the inside you see every room beautifully furnished.

Some people still hold the old religious beliefs that anything beautiful and comfortable is sinful and that God favors the poor over the rich. This isn't true. As Soul becomes a co-creator in the worlds of God, It learns to fend for Itself and do it well. We, as Soul, learn to take care of our obligations, provide for our family, and so on. This is how it works.

*As Soul becomes a co-creator in the worlds of God, It learns to fend for Itself and do it well.*

## CREATIVE DREAMING

Some people do it better than others because they realize that dreams alone will not take them anywhere, not even to the Kingdom of God. You cannot just dream. Life is a combination of dreaming and then making plans to fulfill those dreams. The creative imagination, a gift given to us by God, gives us a way to make our dreams come true.

A spiritually directed person makes sure that his dreams benefit life around him. They aren't selfish dreams that take from the world without ever giving back — that is a life lived with greed and self-interest and is certainly devoid of love. But one person may be comfortable in a mansion while another may be just as comfortable in a cottage.

The ECK Master Rebazar Tarzs lives in a hut, but not because he's poor or because he feels it's wrong to live in good surroundings. He can go to lavish surroundings when he wants to. But he finds that his body — like his residence — is simply a place to be, a place to stay to protect him from the elements. But it must be a good shelter. It must accomplish the purpose of protection and be a place to live, a place to be.

Our thoughts are shaped very easily when we're young. One of the features I enjoy about the video arcades is that so many young people can be found there. And I don't necessarily mean young in years — the people I run into are often youthful well into their seventies and beyond. They are drawn to the video arcades by the technology of today, which gives them a view toward tomorrow. It helps them dream.

## FREE RIDES

I have a reluctance about giving alms to beggars. Concepts about ECK Masters aside, I personally look things over very carefully. To give people something they haven't asked for, or that they want but don't really need, encourages bad habits. It can also deprive your own family of basic necessities.

If I give at the wrong time and it teaches people to rely on others for their welfare, what have I done to their creative imagination? I've put it to sleep.

Social welfare is a program intended to help people. But it's a spiritually blind program in that very little effort is made to discriminate between those who really need help and those who don't.

Social welfare is sometimes used as a politician's ticket to office. Since more people are poor than rich, a candidate can reap a lot more votes by promising to give somebody else's money so those who vote for him can live better. But to teach people to believe that they can get something for nothing does a terrible disservice to their creative imagination: It puts out the Light of Soul.

I am not referring to the disabled and others who are truly in need, or to the elderly who have worked and contributed to a system, whether national or

*To teach people to believe that they can get something for nothing does a terrible disservice to their creative imagination: It puts out the Light of Soul.*

private, for their retirement. This is all right. This is necessary. What I'm talking about are people who take a free ride on the money earned and paid by others, simply because it's easy to get from the officials who run the system.

The officials encourage this attitude out of self-interest. If there aren't enough people asking for the service, then fewer bureaucrats are needed to service them.

And so you have a huge deadness developing in a society. England has tried to turn it around through Margaret Thatcher. Conditions in America might have to grow even worse before it is fully realized that you cannot hand everything to people and not require them to earn their own way. You can't do this without destroying the nation.

*Conditions in America might have to grow even worse before it is fully realized that you cannot hand everything to people and not require them to earn their own way.*

## WORK ETHIC

A lot of fun is made of the Protestant work ethic, but there is something to be said for it. We have changed from an agricultural to an industrial to an information society. Yet there is as valid a way to work today as there was in the past.

At one time most people were farmers. Day after day they worked in the fields, raising the crops, bringing in the grain for their family, tending their cattle—all so they and a few others might have food.

Then we entered the industrial age. People left the fields and went to work on the production lines. Soon after that we had automobiles to make life easier. We could go farther, see and do more, transport food and grain longer distances. Our society became more specialized.

Countries that have handled the aspect of providing for the material needs of humanity are now moving into the information area. Computers and various information services are another way in which people can use their creative imagination to work, learn, and grow.

A person develops spiritual knowledge and wisdom through the experience of doing. You cannot gain spiritual knowledge and wisdom by living off other people, without ever having done anything to earn your own way or contribute to the system that you are part of.

*A person develops spiritual knowledge and wisdom through the experience of doing.*

## PAYING BACK THE QUARTER

Recently I was leaving a video arcade in Minnesota. It looked like it was about to rain. A teenage girl of fifteen or sixteen left her friends and came up to me. "Could you lend me a quarter?" she asked.

It worked in her favor that she wasn't very adept at public begging, but still, I didn't feel inclined to make it too easy for her. "What's it for?" I inquired.

"I need it to call home," she said.

"Or another video game?" I asked, just like a father. I have a daughter—I know how these things work.

"No, really, I need it to call home."

I could see what happened. Absorbed in playing the video games with her friends, she had put her last quarter in the machine. Now she realized it was going to rain, and if she couldn't reach her parents, she'd have to walk home. Not that she couldn't have walked, of course, but she didn't want to; the rain messes up the hair and makes the stuff around the eyes run.

"OK," I finally said, "here's a quarter." She thanked me and started to walk away. "Wait, there's one more thing," I said. This was a delayed reaction on my part. She turned around reluctantly, probably wondering if the quarter was worth it. Would she now have to endure a sermon?

I said, "If you ever feel that it's important to pay back this quarter, then give it to one of the younger kids here. But don't make them feel as if they owe it to you."

The puzzled expression on her face was beautiful to see, because she was being opened up to a new principle. She got what she had asked for. And at the same time she was made aware that it came with a responsibility to give back a gift to life. But it has to be given with no strings attached. I left her with this paradox in the shape of a little quarter.

Kids in video parlors are always asking for money, and I rarely give it to them because it sends out the wrong message. But this young lady seemed pretty sharp. The words alone may not have been enough to get the point across to her. But if she remembers how I dealt with her, she'll figure it out in time. Someday a little kid will ask her, "Do you have a quarter?" Maybe she'll give it to him and remember to say, "OK. Now if you ever feel it's important to pay back this quarter, then give it to someone else, but don't make them feel as if they owe it to you."

That may be a pretty heavy load to place on a teenager, but I think she can handle it. Either that, or she'll never ask a stranger for money again. Or if she does, it won't be me.

## TIPS

Money can be very useful, but when it is used wrongly, it develops the worst habits in people. I can accept that money is used as a way to say thank you, such as leaving a tip for the waiter. It's part of the system. Besides that, if you expect to dine in that

*She got what she had asked for. And at the same time she was made aware that it came with a responsibility to give back a gift to life.*

*Money can be very useful, but when it is used wrongly, it develops the worst habits in people.*

place again and get any kind of service from him, you would be wise to leave a tip. Why? Because it's the custom.

If you don't go along with it, nobody actually holds up a sign that says, "You have not honored this custom. Shame, shame." But the waiter, in his own way, lets you know that you have broken an invisible law. The next time you come in, he might accidentally spill a tray of food on you as a way of saying, "Here's to you, friend." This is how customs are built.

Tips are handled differently in Europe than in America. People from other countries think we Americans are foolish to throw away 15 or 20 percent at a time, but that's our custom. It's as binding on us as the European custom of having a gratuity added to your bill and just leaving a few coins for the waiter.

As we work within a system, we have to know our way around. People who travel should learn what is expected as a favor for service in each country they visit. But if they miss the mark, there's no great harm done, no great loss. We do our best, but we also have to keep in mind that everything in life doesn't have the same consequence. Some things are minor; some things are very important.

*We do our best, but we also have to keep in mind that everything in life doesn't have the same consequence.*

## ECK Fortune Cookies

The teenager in the video arcade did not recognize it, of course, but she had the experience of a waking dream. Had she been able to perceive it more vividly, it would have been what I call the Golden-tongued Wisdom.

The Golden-tongued Wisdom is a more direct way in which the ECK speaks to an individual. It comes in some way that you can hear or see, usually through the voice of another person or through the written

The Golden-tongued Wisdom is like a Chinese fortune cookie from the ECK.

word. Its purpose is to give specific directions on how to arrange your life in a more spiritual way. The Golden-tongued Wisdom is like a Chinese fortune cookie from the ECK.

## LOVE THEIR FAULTS

An ECK initiate told me about her experience with the Golden-tongued Wisdom. It happened as a result of her interaction with a person at work.

Strange as it seems, there are some people in this world who form friendships by making fun of people. And stranger still is that the friends put up with it. Maybe that's what friends are for.

I noticed this trait in an old friend that I hadn't seen for many years. We had been in the service together. He's a salesman now, and maybe that accounts for his banter. His idea of conversation is to put others down with mild insults about the way they look, how they dress, and what they say. But it's all done in the spirit of good-natured ribbing—or humor.

This female ECK initiate worked with a man who constantly found fault with her. He liked to insult her in a light, friendly way, as co-workers tend to do.

One day the ECKist, her husband, and another friend went to a restaurant with this man and his wife. During the meal her co-worker began with his usual "friendly" put-downs, but this time she'd had it. She just couldn't take it anymore.

Normally a quiet, soft-spoken person who rarely shows anger, she blew her stack. "If you couldn't insult me, you wouldn't be able to think of one thing to say!"

The man was quite shocked, but she wasn't finished. She worked herself into such a state of anger that she got louder and louder, until every eye in the restaurant was turned toward them. In other words, she embarrassed the whole table.

After the other couple left, the ECKist, her husband, and their friend talked for a while in the parking lot. "You had a right to defend yourself," they reassured her. "If he can dish it out, he should be able to take it."

While they talked, her attention was drawn to a license plate enclosed in one of those steel frames. She tried to listen to the conversation, but her eyes kept returning to the bottom part of the frame. Imprinted on it were the words *love their faults.*

"Maybe this will teach him a lesson," her friend said.

*Love their faults,* she thought, staring at the license plate.

"You were perfectly justified," her husband said.

*Love their faults,* she read again. What was it about that license plate?

Finally it hit her, and she started to laugh. Her husband and their friend couldn't figure out how she had gotten over her anger so suddenly. "Look at that license plate," she said. "The ECK is trying to tell us something."

What they saw was the complete message: "Geologists love their faults." The ECKist had been reading only the words on the bottom part of the frame.

## ACTING WITH LOVE

Even though she had good reason to call the coworker to task, she felt she could have done it with love instead of anger. To act with anger is to act from a state of power.

When we act with love, we allow the other person to understand how we feel. We let him know that we realize he is not necessarily bad, but we do not want him to practice that sort of behavior on us in the

*When we act with love, we allow the other person to understand how we feel.*

future or he will lose our friendship. It's clean and unemotional, and it takes the anger out of it. This kind of love is the charity that is spoken of in the Christian Bible.

## CLEAREST EXPRESSIONS

I try to be careful of the words I use when the talk is being translated simultaneously into different languages. A few years ago I discovered that the translators found it difficult to convey my American colloquialisms.

I have found that the English spoken in Nigeria is quite different from the English spoken in America, Europe, or Singapore. Though it comes from the mother tongue which originated in England, it's a very different English. The expressions used in Africa are poetic. The people mix the poetry of their own culture with the stiffness of the English language, and the result is the most beautiful English I have ever heard.

To learn how to express myself in the clearest way possible, I got one of those computer programs which check one's grammar. As I write for the ECK, the program actually gives me grades. I find this very useful. My writings not only go out to many countries which speak various versions of English, they must also be translated into other languages. If I can write and speak in clear images, it is easier for the translator than if I get into abstract mental concepts which require a complicated explanation.

*I too am working as the creative dreamer, trying to carry forth my dream of you as the enlightened Soul.*

## AN AID TO SOUL

I too am working as the creative dreamer, trying to carry forth my dream of you as the enlightened Soul. The computer program is one of the many aids that Soul—you and I—manifests to help us to communicate with each other. But it can only do so much. Once the computer gives me a score on an article I have written, it is up to me to figure out how to adjust it to the specific readership I'm trying to reach.

The computer program also points out the use of too many adjectives. No one wants to read about "the most wonderful, delightful, exotic" anything. By the time you get through it, you feel you've gotten too much fat with your meat. There's too much weight in all the wrong places.

We have to watch out for spiritual weight in the wrong places too. This means we have to be more careful about the things we say and do; otherwise the weight goes on in the wrong places. The weight, of course, is karma.

*We have to watch out for spiritual weight in the wrong places too. The weight, of course, is karma.*

## COMMUNICATION SKILLS

The English language is very much alive in America. The problem is, it changes so rapidly that it becomes almost a foreign language from one generation to the next. People in their forties and fifties use colloquial expressions that seem very natural to them. But when they speak to their teenagers, the kids wonder where on earth their parents ever found such faded, useless language.

No wonder there is a generation gap. Teenagers usually think very loosely about life. Their dreams involve dating or learning to drive. That's old stuff to the parents. They can't appreciate dreams that do not translate into important things, like owning a home.

Teenagers, on the other hand, cannot appreciate their parents' concern about orderliness. When a mother says, "Clean up your room," she's referring to the mess that covers the entire floor, bed, dresser, and everywhere else. What she means is, fold your clothes, put everything on shelves and in drawers, sweep the floor, dust the furniture, and make the room look disgustingly antiseptic.

The teenager looks at the very same mess, thinks she means, "You must make a path to the bed," and proceeds to kick aside the debris until a pathway forms.

The parent comes back to check the room and explodes: "I told you to clean up this mess!" "But I did," the teenager insists, concluding that you simply cannot talk to these people. Parent and child love each other—or they will again once the teenage years have passed—but for now there is an inability to communicate with each other.

> We have to use creative imagination to communicate with people.

If this goes on between people who live under the same roof, is it any wonder that we have to use so much creative imagination to communicate with people at work and outside our homes? It's the same kind of difficulty that countries have in communicating their values and customs to one another.

## MISSIONARY EFFORTS

When a certain country has a bit of missionary spirit, too bad for the neighbors. The zealous will try to push new customs and beliefs on everybody else, whether they want them or not.

This is a great miscommunication, and it generally springs from ignorance. It starts with an attitude: I belong to the best religion (or political party). It's my duty to convince everyone who is committed to any other thought system to see things my way— or else.

This is what happens when power enters into the missionary spirit. If love compels a missionary effort, you tell people what they ask about truth, and that's all. You don't tell them more than they ask, because then you're moving out of the love state and switching to the power state. You're telling them something they have no need for, do not want to hear, and definitely do not want pushed upon them.

So often we can see where a missionary effort stands on the spiritual scale by how hard the missionary pushes his beliefs on those who do not want them. His justification is that he wants to save the unbeliever's Soul. "I'm doing it for the love of God," he claims.

This type of missionary doesn't realize that the love of God would not invalidate his neighbor's individuality. That person needs his freedom. You cannot show love for God by stealing another's freedom. This is something we must always keep in mind in our ECK missionary work.

*You cannot show love for God by stealing another's freedom.*

## YOUR ABILITY TO DREAM

Why do we dream? Why is it important to dream? Because dreaming comes from the creative imagination, which is God's gift to you and to me. It is the nature of immortal Soul to dream. This is why your dreams, both in everyday life and while asleep, are so important.

*Your dreams, both in everyday life and while asleep, are so important.*

Through your ability to dream, you often have experiences in the other worlds where you act as an observer. But as you move farther along in ECK, you become the participant in your dreams. You become the actor.

You begin to see goals, spiritual goals which may be as valid as finding a home for your family. You want a place where they can be happy, a haven away from the fast pace of today's society. You create a warm place where friends are welcome.

*Dream.
Dream your
way home.
Dream your
way back
to God.*

It's a place where you can go, a home, a spiritual dream. Because as we plan our homes, whether it's a rented home or one we buy, we're just thinking of a higher home. It's the home of Soul. The place where Soul has come from, from the heart of God in the Ocean of Love and Mercy.

Dream. Dream your way home. Dream your way back to God. Use your creative imagination, because that's the only way you can return to the source of all life.

I would like to give you my blessings on your journey home, today and forever. May the blessings be.

*ECK European Seminar, The Hague, Netherlands,
Sunday, July 30, 1989*

# GLOSSARY

Words set in SMALL CAPS are defined elsewhere in this glossary.

ARAHATA.    An experienced and qualified teacher for ECKANKAR classes.

CHELA.    A spiritual student.

ECK.    The Life Force, the Holy Spirit, or Audible Life Current which sustains all life.

ECKANKAR.    Religion of the Light and Sound of God. Also known as the Ancient Science of SOUL TRAVEL. A truly spiritual religion for the individual in modern times, known as the secret path to God via dreams and SOUL TRAVEL. The teachings provide a framework for anyone to explore their own spiritual experiences. Established by Paul Twitchell, the modern-day founder, in 1965.

ECK MASTERS.    Spiritual Masters who can assist and protect people in their spiritual studies and travels. The ECK Masters are from a long line of God-Realized SOULS who know the responsibility that goes with spiritual freedom.

HU.    The most ancient, secret name for God. The singing of the word HU, pronounced like the word *hue,* is considered a love song to God. It is sung in the ECK Worship Service.

INITIATION.    Earned by the ECK member through spiritual unfoldment and service to God. The initiation is a private ceremony in which the individual is linked to the Sound and Light of God.

LIVING ECK MASTER.    The title of the spiritual leader of ECKANKAR. His duty is to lead SOULS back to God. The Living ECK Master can assist spiritual students physically as the Outer Master, in the dream state as the Dream Master, and in the spiritual worlds as the Inner Master. Sri Harold Klemp became the MAHANTA, the Living ECK Master in 1981.

MAHANTA.   A title to describe the highest state of God Consciousness on earth, often embodied in the LIVING ECK MASTER. He is the Living Word.

PLANES.   The levels of heaven, such as the Astral, Causal, Mental, Etheric, and Soul planes.

SATSANG.   A class in which students of ECK study a monthly lesson from ECKANKAR.

THE SHARIYAT-KI-SUGMAD.   The sacred scriptures of ECKANKAR. The scriptures are comprised of twelve volumes in the spiritual worlds. The first two were transcribed from the inner PLANES by Paul Twitchell, modern-day founder of ECKANKAR.

SOUL.   The True Self. The inner, most sacred part of each person. Soul exists before birth and lives on after the death of the physical body. As a spark of God, Soul can see, know, and perceive all things. It is the creative center of Its own world.

SOUL TRAVEL.   The expansion of consciousness. The ability of SOUL to transcend the physical body and travel into the spiritual worlds of God. Soul Travel is taught only by the LIVING ECK MASTER. It helps people unfold spiritually and can provide proof of the existence of God and life after death.

SOUND AND LIGHT OF ECK.   The Holy Spirit. The two aspects through which God appears in the lower worlds. People can experience them by looking and listening within themselves and through SOUL TRAVEL.

SPIRITUAL EXERCISES OF ECK.   The daily practice of certain techniques to get us in touch with the Light and Sound of God.

SUGMAD.   A sacred name for God. Sugmad is neither masculine nor feminine; It is the source of all life.

WAH Z.   The spiritual name of Sri Harold Klemp. It means the Secret Doctrine. It is his name in the spiritual worlds.

# INDEX

237

# For Further Reading and Study*

## Journey of Soul
### Mahanta Transcripts, Book 1
Harold Klemp

This collection of talks by Eckankar's spiritual leader shows how to apply the unique Spiritual Exercises of ECK—dream exercises, visualizations, and Soul Travel methods—to unlock your natural abilities as Soul. Learn how to hear the little-known Sounds of God and follow Its Light for practical daily guidance and upliftment.

## The Spiritual Exercises of ECK
Harold Klemp

This book is a staircase with 131 steps. It's a special staircase, because you don't have to climb all the steps to get to the top. Each step is a spiritual exercise, a way to help you explore your inner worlds. And what awaits you at the top? The doorway to spiritual freedom, self-mastery, wisdom, and love.

## 35 Golden Keys to Who You Are & Why You're Here
Linda C. Anderson

Discover thirty-five golden keys to mastering your spiritual destiny through the ancient teachings of Eckankar, Religion of the Light and Sound of God. The dramatic, true stories in this book equal anything found in the spiritual literature of today. Learn ways to immediately bring more love, peace, and purpose to your life.

## How to Master Change in Your Life: Sixty-seven Ways to Handle Life's Toughest Moments
Mary Carroll Moore

In your life, you always have a choice. You can flee from change, a victim of *fate*. Or, as the hero, you can embrace each challenge you face with courage and grace. Included are sixty-seven powerful techniques to help you understand change, plan the future, conquer fear and worry, and resolve problems of the past.

**\*Available at your local bookstore.** If unavailable, call (612) 544-0066. Or write: ECKANKAR Books, P.O. Box 27300, Minneapolis, MN 55427 U.S.A.

# There May Be an Eckankar Study Group near You

Eckankar offers a variety of local and international activities for the spiritual seeker. With hundreds of study groups worldwide, Eckankar is near you! Many areas have Eckankar centers where you can browse through the books in a quiet, unpressured environment, talk with others who share an interest in this ancient teaching, and attend beginning discussion classes on how to gain the attributes of Soul: wisdom, power, love, and freedom.

Around the world, Eckankar study groups offer special one-day or weekend seminars on the basic teachings of Eckankar. Check your phone book under **ECKANKAR**, or call **(612) 544-0066** for membership information and the location of the Eckankar center or study group nearest you. Or write **ECKANKAR, Att: Information, P.O. Box 27300, Minneapolis, MN 55427 U.S.A.**

☐ Please send me information on the nearest Eckankar center or study group in my area.

☐ Please send me more information about membership in Eckankar, which includes a twelve-month spiritual study.

Please type or print clearly                                                    940

Name _____
    first (given)                          last (family)

Street_____ Apt. # _____

City _____ State/Prov. _____

ZIP/Postal Code _____ Country _____

# About the Author

Sri Harold Klemp was born in Wisconsin and grew up on a small farm. He attended a two-room country schoolhouse before going to high school at a religious boarding school in Milwaukee, Wisconsin.

After preministerial college in Milwaukee and Fort Wayne, Indiana, he enlisted in the U.S. Air Force. There he trained as a language specialist at Indiana University and a radio intercept operator at Goodfellow AFB, Texas. Then followed a two-year stint in Japan where he first encountered Eckankar.

In October 1981, he became the spiritual leader of Eckankar, Religion of the Light and Sound of God. His full title is Sri Harold Klemp, the Mahanta, the Living ECK Master. As the Living ECK Master, Harold Klemp is responsible for the continued evolution of the Eckankar teachings.

His mission is to help people find their way back to God in this life. Harold Klemp travels to ECK seminars in North America, Europe, and the South Pacific. He has also visited Africa and many countries throughout the world, meeting with spiritual seekers and giving inspirational talks. There are many videocassettes and audiocassettes of his public talks available.

In his talks and writings, Harold Klemp's sense of humor and practical approach to spirituality have helped many people around the world find truth in their lives and greater inner freedom, wisdom, and love.

*International Who's Who of Intellectuals*
*Ninth Edition*